MALINGERING AND DECEPTION
IN ADOLESCENTS

MALINGERING AND DECEPTION IN ADOLESCENTS:

ASSESSING CREDIBILITY
IN CLINICAL AND FORENSIC SETTINGS

JOSEPH T. McCANN, PsyD, JD

American Psychological Association, Washington, DC

For these reasons, I have maintained an interest in the clinical evaluation of malingering and other forms of deception. With much greater frequency, the subject of these clinical and forensic evaluations has been a teenager, yet I have found a disturbingly limited amount of research on the topic of malingering and deception in adolescents. The issues pertaining to dissimulation in these cases often had to be conceptualized by extrapolating findings from research on adults, or by using child development research that had been conducted on related issues such as moral reasoning or development of the ability to lie.

While undertaking the writing of this book, I have tried to remain fully aware that there is very little empirical research available on this topic. However, I have accumulated a considerable amount of clinical material that provides interesting insight into how adolescents modify their self-reports either consciously or unconsciously. Although the lack of extensive research initially created ambivalence for me in deciding whether to write a book on adolescent malingering at this time, I found more material than I originally thought I would. Ultimately, I decided that the importance of the problem could not be ignored, and I moved forward with the project.

Much of this text is based both on clinical case material and on existing research on child development and adult malingering, to the extent that the latter is relevant to adolescent populations. The call for more research is often a standard part of any scholarly endeavor, but this recommendation is particularly apt with respect to adolescent malingering and deception. Also, I have deliberately avoided covering the issue of true versus false allegations of sexual abuse in any detail because this topic has been covered in several excellent texts on the subject (Ceci & Bruck, 1995; Kuehnle, 1996; Ney, 1995). I drew upon and referenced the material from this literature to the degree that it helps to inform the general practice of assessing malingering and deception among adolescent populations.

A brief comment is also in order about the case examples that are presented in the text. All of the material is drawn from actual cases, and every effort has been made to provide the necessary detail to highlight issues and concepts discussed in the text. I have created pseudonyms where names are used, and some of the details have been altered in order to protect the confidentiality and privacy of the individuals involved. However, I believe the cases are an accurate portrayal of the issues often encountered in both clinical and forensic practice.

these two individuals know how much I value their friendship, I hope they now know the extent of my respect and gratitude.

I wish to express additional thanks to the staff at APA Books, and to Julia Frank-McNeil and Mary Lynn Skutley in particular. Their flexibility and openness to the idea for this book made working with their staff a pleasure. A special acknowledgment is owed to Beth Beisel at APA Books, who provided a thorough and extremely helpful review of the manuscript. Her comments and suggestions reflected the highest level of professionalism and competence, and her input served only to improve the final product; any shortcomings in the final product are my responsibility alone. I would also like to thank Valerie Montenegro for her excellent copyediting of the manuscript; her efforts also reflect the highest level of professionalism.

Finally, the completion of this book is due in large measure to the encouragement and support of my wife, Michele Ries McCann. She could always be relied on to show interest in the progress I was making, to give an honest critique, and to provide the loving support she always so readily gives. I am truly indebted to her for the way she pleasantly accepted the countless hours I spent at my desk and the numerous times she was awakened in the middle of the night as I was coming to bed after I had finished writing for the day. And although he is a bit too young yet to realize it, my son, Alexander, had a special part in the completion of this work. I needed to complete the manuscript before his arrival into the world; if not for him, I might still be trying to complete this book.

1

The Significance of Malingering and Deception in Adolescents

At one time or another, most people have had firsthand experience with a child who has claimed to be sick in order to avoid having to go to school. A concern of parents and school officials is the degree to which such claims of illness are genuine or feigned. This familiar occurrence constitutes one of the more obvious instances in which the veracity of a child's self-reports are questioned.

Over the past several years, mental health professionals have become increasingly concerned about the veracity of an individual's claim of physical or psychological disturbance. Although there are a few exceptions, most of the literature has focused on the assessment of malingering and feigning in adults (cf. Rogers, 1997). Nevertheless, there has been an increasing need for mental health services among adolescent populations, and consequently, the need for evaluating the veracity of adolescents' claims of psychological and physical disturbance has increased. Thus, there is a need for applying reliable, valid, and practical methods for assessing malingering and deception among adolescent populations.

Although lying and cheating are frequently associated with delinquent and antisocial youths, these behaviors are quite common among children with no history of mental health treatment. Achenbach (1985) noted that lying and cheating occur in 23% of 4- to 5-year-olds and gradually decline to a prevalence of 15% in 16-year-olds. Although these percentages represent parents' self-reports of problematic behavior in their children, it is highly likely that the percentage of children lying or cheating at some point in their lives is much greater than the percentages cited by Achenbach.

The issue of deception is not limited to any one setting and is a substantial problem in general clinical practice. The prevalence of malingering, which is the intentional feigning of symptoms to achieve some secondary gain, is quite significant. Yates, Nordquist, and Schultz-Ross (1996) found that 13% of patients seen in a psychiatric emergency room were either strongly or definitely suspected of malingering. This percentage is consistent with a 15% prevalence rate cited by Rogers, Sewell, and Goldstein (1994). Moreover, Rogers, Hinds, and Sewell (1996) estimated that this 15% prevalence rate is applicable to adolescent clinical settings. Whereas these rates reflect the number of patients believed to be malingering, the issue of possible feigning or dissimulation of psychiatric illness is typically considered, at least as a rule out diagnosis, in most mental health evaluations.

The veracity of adolescent self-reports has become an important broad-based focus for a number of reasons. The controversy of true versus false accusations of child sexual abuse has prompted extensive professional debate and has stimulated a growing body of scientific research on the capacity of child witnesses to testify relevantly and accurately about claims of abuse. Although the debate over the truthfulness of sexual abuse allegations has given a "black eye" to the mental health profession (Fox, 1995), it has also raised important questions about the ability of psychologists, judges, child welfare workers, and other professionals to determine the veracity and truthfulness of a child or adolescent's self-reports.

Other reasons for increased interest in the truthfulness of adolescent self-reports are related to the rising number of teenagers involved in the criminal justice system. It is generally assumed that defendants in the criminal justice system are more prone to deliberately distort information or feign mental illness or some disability in order to obtain leniency in the form of a reduced sentence, acquittal, or other favorable treatment. Thus, the issue of malingering and deceptive processes is of primary importance when evaluating anyone involved as a defendant in criminal courts, and in light of recent trends, this is particularly true for adolescents. Statistics show that although violent crime has been consistently decreasing overall, the general numbers mask an alarming rise in violent crime among adolescents. From 1988 to 1992, the arrest rate for violent crime has increased 45% for juveniles. More specifically, arrests have increased 52% for murder, 17% for rape, 49% for robbery, and 47% for aggravated assault (Federal Bureau of Investigation, 1993). The level of serious and violent crime is increasing among children and adolescents, both in the rate of juvenile offenders (Osgood, O'Malley, Bachman, & Johnston, 1989) and in the rate of juvenile victims of violence (Hammond & Yung, 1993; Tolan, Guerra, & Kendall, 1995b).

These trends are relatively recent and do not reflect the long-standing concerns over adolescent self-reports that clinicians have had while treating adolescent psychological disturbances. In particular, teenage populations have traditionally presented problems for clinicians because of the resistance, denial, and sarcasm that members of this age group often exhibit in psychotherapy. Therefore, the issue of deception and truthfulness in clinical treatment of adolescents has been and continues to be significant.

This book will provide practitioners with techniques and methods for assessing various forms of malingering and deception in both clinical and forensic settings. The remainder of this chapter will outline some of the reasons that these issues have become so important and will provide a context in which to understand the problem.

SOCIAL FACTORS THAT ENGENDER MALINGERING AND DECEPTION

Several social factors have contributed to changes in the way adolescents must cope with their environment and the way society views the teenage years. Many of these factors emphasize the need to have useful and accurate methods for evaluating the veracity of adolescent self-reports.

Adolescents' Involvement in the Courts

An increasing number of adolescents are becoming involved in the criminal justice system by way of their involvement in a variety of criminal activities. Among the many proposals and suggestions that have been offered to address the growing tide of violent juvenile offenders is to effectively identify those adolescents who may respond to intervention such as placement or psychological treatment and to distinguish those who can be helped from the smaller group of serious, persistent, and repeat offenders who cannot be rehabilitated (Wilson & Howell, 1994). These suggestions are consistent with a major factor distinguishing the juvenile criminal justice system from the adult system: There is an assumption more prevalent within the juvenile system that criminal offenders can be treated in a therapeutic environment. Thus, the juvenile system is generally more rehabilitative, whereas the adult criminal justice system is guided by a philosophy of incapacitation of offenders and retribution that seeks to punish those who commit serious and violent crimes (Melton, Petrila, Poythress, & Slobogin, 1987; Mnookin & Weisberg, 1989). Despite these philosophical differences between the adult and juvenile justice systems, recent findings have suggested that there is essentially little or no difference in the severity of sentences imposed on juveniles adjudicated in the juvenile system versus those adjudicated in the adult system (Kinder, Veneziano, Fichter, & Axuma, 1995). Moreover, this research found that transfer of juveniles to adult status does not appear to deter juvenile violent crime, except for a small portion of juvenile offenders.

Given the alarming rise of violent offending among adolescents, there has been an increase in the number of cases adjudicated in the juvenile system. Mental health professionals are more frequently being asked to evaluate juvenile offenders to answer a variety of questions, including amenability to treatment, prospects for rehabilitation by a specified age, and risk of violence.

Child Abuse

The twentieth century has witnessed a gradual and steady increase in the number of laws, social programs, and pervasive views in society that have as their main goal the protection of children. Restrictions on the use of corporal punishment in schools and mandated child abuse reporting laws are examples of how society has shown greater concern for the welfare of children and adolescents. More specifically, increasing attention is being paid to the prevention of child physical and sexual abuse; consequently, there has been a focus on the veracity and truthfulness of children's claims of abuse. Reflecting the importance of this issue is a mounting body of research into the truthfulness of children's claims of sexual abuse (Gardner, 1992; Kuehnle, 1996; Myers, 1995; Ney, 1995; Schacter, Kagan, & Leichtman, 1995) and children's credibility and accuracy as witnesses in courtrooms (cf. Ceci & Bruck, 1993; Goodman & Bottoms, 1993).

Closely connected to this issue of true versus false claims of child sexual abuse has been the phenomenon of parents' deliberately inducing physical or psychological symptoms in their children in order to assume the role of a patient vicariously through their children. This condition has been called Munchausen Syndrome by Proxy, or Factitious Disorder by Proxy (Forsyth, 1991). Evidence of the rise in interest given to this syndrome is found in the introduction of this condition into the appendix of Criteria Sets and Axes Provided for Further Study in the fourth edition of the *Diagnostic and Statistical Manual of Mental Disorders* (*DSM-IV*; American Psychiatric Association, 1994). The clinical features associated with this syndrome constitute a form of child abuse because of the fact that the children in these cases are deliberately inflicted with some medical condition, usually by the child's mother, so that the parent can attain, by proxy, the role of a patient. In chapter 7, I will cover this disorder in more detail.

Greater emphasis in recent years on promoting child welfare has brought with it the collateral issue of determining which child self-reports are valid, which suggest feigning of symptoms, and which are the product of coaching or parental influences. As a result, clinicians have been forced to confront issues of the truthfulness of child and adolescent self-reports, thus making the topic centrally relevant to clinical and forensic practice.

Divorce Proceedings

Greater sensitivity to the welfare of children is evident in family law also. When disputes arise over child custody in divorce proceedings, courts invariably use the standard "best interests of the child" in determining what happens to the children (Goldstein, Freud, Solnit, & Goldstein, 1986; Melton et al., 1987). In some jurisdictions, children have even been given more expanded rights in that they have been able to bring suit to "divorce their parents," demand placement with specific foster parents, or in some other way have an active voice in deciding what happens to them.

In highly conflicted child custody cases, there is potential for deception as well. One parent may attempt to alienate the child from the other parent by various tactics, one of which is to encourage the child to raise an allegation of sexual abuse (Mikkelsen, Gutheil, & Emens, 1992). In some cases, the child may be encouraged, or "forced" out of feelings of obligation, to go along with the allegation to maintain secure attachments with at least one parent. The increased prevalence of divorce in this country has led to a greater number of disputes over child custody. Moreover, the role of mental health professionals in assisting courts with making decisions about child custody has increased. As a result, there is a greater need to have methods for evaluating in individual cases, for example, whether an adolescent's claim of allegiance to a particular parent is based on legitimate issues, whether there has been parental programming, or whether there are attempts by the adolescent to have custody assigned to a parent who can be more easily manipulated.

Modern Treatment Considerations

In the past decade, there have been a number of significant changes in the way that mental health services are provided. The role of managed care has expanded to the degree that clinicians have been forced to justify their treatment plans and to establish the efficacy of their interventions. Moreover, consumers of mental health services have found that their access to treatment is often limited or denied and there is no guarantee that insurance will provide coverage. As a result, it is now important in the age of shrinking resources to make sure that those who genuinely need treatment receive it and that those who do not are readily identified.

These changes in the mental health system have occurred along with an increase in the focus on adolescent mental health services. Specialized adolescent psychiatric hospitals have proliferated in recent years, and many communities have a need for acute psychiatric inpatient facilities to cope with the large influx of more severe adolescent disturbances into the system. In light of the concurrent rise in adolescent treatment programs and the need to allocate resources to those who need care, there is a rising demand not only in forensic settings but also in clinical treatment to distinguish bona fide clinical symptomatology from claims that are feigned. In other words, clinicians and therapists also need to have methods for evaluating the veracity of adolescent self-reports.

TYPES OF DECEPTION

In general, deceptive forms of behavior can take rather mild forms such as occasional "fibs" or lies, or they can be more extreme such as chronic lying, deliberate feigning of physical or emotional distress, cheating or conning others out of money, or making false allegations (e.g., of sexual abuse). The term *deception* is actually a more palatable reference to *lying,* which is defined as "an assertion of something known or believed by the speaker to be untrue, *with intent to deceive*" (Ekman, 1985; Sigmon & Snyder, 1993; emphasis added). The key to this definition is found in the speaker's intent or motivation to make a statement that is not true. An individual can utter a false statement by repeating it to another. However, such statements as untrue rumors or mistaken beliefs are distinguished from lying or deception in that they do not involve an intent on the part of the speaker to deceive or mislead the person to whom the statement is being uttered. In studying forms of deceptive

7

behavior, underlying motives, intent, and the context in which the statement is made are all crucial pieces of information that must be considered. Table 1.1 outlines various distinctions that can be drawn between true statements, lies, mistaken beliefs, and more benign forms of deception. The implication of these distinguishing factors is that assessing truthfulness involves several dimensions, including the speaker's intent and motivation, the setting or context in which a statement is made, and the expectation of the recipient of the statement.

One of the primary images that is evoked when the issue of deception first arises is an adolescent who has been caught for some misbehavior and faces punishment. In less severe situations, teenagers will often minimize their actions or distort the truth to avoid being punished by their parents. When the consequences are more severe, such as when adolescents face legal punishment before a court, there is strong motivation to deny, minimize, or in some other way distort self-reports. Therefore, motivation and context are important assessment considerations, as subsequent discussions will illustrate.

DEVELOPMENT OF LYING AND DECEPTION

Although this text deals solely with deceptive processes in adolescents in clinical and forensic settings, it is important to have some understanding of how these processes develop. Research from developmental psychology is informative and contributes to the understanding of how and why adolescents may lie and what role such behavior has in their lives. The ability to lie and engage in deceptive behavior is established very early in life. By the age of three, children are capable of telling a lie (Lewis, 1993; Lewis, Stanger, & Sullivan, 1989). To be capable of lying, the child must have "knowledge of himself [sic], knowledge of his own mind, knowledge of the other's mind, and knowledge that the other has knowledge of his mind" (Lewis, 1993, p. 103). Thus, development of the ability to deceive is dependent on corresponding developmental changes in cognitive skills in children. One important distinction to be drawn, however, is that very young children are not

Table 1.1

Distinctions Between Truths, Lies, False Beliefs, and Innocent Deception

	Category			
	Truth	Lie	False belief	Innocent deception
Statement:	True	False	False	False
Speaker believes statement is:	True	False	True	False
Speaker intends statement to be:	Truthful	Deceitful	Truthful	Deceitful
Speaker wants to convey:	Truthfulness	Truthfulness	Truthfulness	Deceitfulness
Speaker's motive:	Good	Bad	Good	Good
Speaker expects listener to:	Believe	Believe	Believe	Not believe
False statement is:	N/A	Intended	Unintended	Intended
Examples	Accurate reports	Lies, hoaxes, "white" lies, hypocrisy	Misperceptions, inaccurate interpretations	Jokes, teasing, irony, sarcasm, hyperbole, understatement, banter

NOTE: Reprinted with permission from "Children's Comprehension of Truths, Lies, and False Beliefs," by N. W. Perry, 1995. In T. Ney (Ed.), *True and False Allegations of Child Sexual Abuse: Assessment and Case Management* (p. 77), New York: Brunner/Mazel. Copyright 1995 by Brunner/Mazel.

Table 1.2

Stages of Moral Development and Their Connection to Truthfulness in Adolescence

Stage	Relevant factors	Implications for truthfulness	Examples in adolescence
I. Preconventional level			
1: Egocentric	Morality is absolute; seek rewards, avoid punishment.	Truths and lies used to obtain reward or avoid punishment.	Psychopathic lies; narcissistic fantasy; antisocial deception.
2: Authority-based	Obedience; morality defined by authority figures.	Truthfulness depends on allegiances to certain people; adhere to external authority.	Being swayed by one parent; symptom coaching.

II. Conventional level

3: Conformity	Morality based on that which gains approval from others.	Statements that please adults or peers.	Lies used to endorse peer group norms.
4: Social order	Morality viewed as rules of "law and order" that make society work.	Truths or lies used to resolve interpersonal conflict; carrying out duties.	Lies used to resolve conflict; obtain desired goal.

III. Postconventional level

5: Social contract	Recognition of different perspectives on morality, each with right to exist.	Truths or lies used to protect human rights and freedoms.	"White lies" to protect friends, parents, etc.
6: Universal ethics	Belief in respect for personal worth; higher order fairness and justice.	Truthfulness acknowledged as way of preserving justice and fairness.	Adherence to personal convictions, beliefs, etc.

17

or hiding emotions), there are other factors such as level of moral reasoning, social contexts, and personal beliefs and attitudes that must be considered when evaluating adolescents.

CLINICAL VERSUS FORENSIC SETTINGS

Although it is helpful to have a developmental and conceptual framework for deceptive forms of behavior, it is also important for mental health professionals to have some appreciation of how their opinions and interventions are used in the specific setting in which they practice. The findings from a psychological evaluation have different implications when they are rendered in a clinical as opposed to a forensic context. Individual practitioners take on different roles and have different purposes when acting as a therapist versus acting as forensic examiner.

The various ways in which clinical and forensic roles differ from one another have been the focus of recent attention (Greenberg & Shuman, 1997; Kuehnle, 1996). Convincing arguments have been made that clinicians should avoid engaging in dual roles of both therapist and forensic evaluator. This delineation of roles readily applies to issues involving the evaluation and treatment of adolescents, regardless of the specific issues being addressed. Several factors distinguish clinical and forensic roles. The ultimate client in clinical settings is the identified adult, adolescent, or child client or family. In forensic settings, practitioners generally serve the judicial system, particularly lawyers or judges. In addition, the goal of clinical services is to understand and treat psychological symptoms and to reduce suffering; forensic settings have as the ultimate goal the gathering and collecting of uncontaminated data. Toward these ends, clinicians typically serve in the role of advocate for the patient, whereas forensic evaluators function as fact finder. In their respective roles, clinicians are supportive of the patient or family, whereas the stance of a forensic examiner is one of neutrality. Another distinction made between clinical and forensic roles involves the assumptions typically made. That is, clinicians generally assume—though not invariably—the trustworthiness of the patient's self-reports. Forensic evaluators must entertain multiple hypotheses, including the likelihood that a particular subject is dissembling or malingering. Finally, clinicians employ strategies and techniques that are therapeutic and bring about relief from symptoms. On the other hand, forensic examiners must use only those techniques that are legally defensible.

Based on this clear delineation of roles that distinguishes treating clinician from forensic evaluator, it should come as no surprise that the relative importance of various approaches to conceptualizing malingering will vary as a function of the particular role one assumes and the setting in which one functions. Thus, deceptive strategies and attempts at feigning may be viewed in clinical treatment settings as presenting symptomatology (e.g., lying), impediments to developing a working relationship, or as an adolescent's means for seeking help from others. In short, the issues of deception in clinical assessment and treatment will have different significance to the clinician than they will for the forensic examiner.

In forensic settings, malingering and deception are typically viewed as significant issues to be addressed in each examination. Originally, the concept of malingering referred to a crime committed within the context of military law; ancient laws viewed the intentional simulation or production of illness or injury to avoid military duties as an offense punishable by death (Mendelson, 1995). Under most current legal systems, malingering is now viewed as an evidentiary issue in which mental illness or psychological disturbances are claimed in criminal or personal injury cases. Expert testimony is usually offered to inform the trier of fact, such as a jury or judge, as to whether or not a criminal defendant or civil plaintiff is malingering or in some other way dissimulating. Moreover, malingering and deception are still actionable offenses when they are undertaken with fraudulent intent. Thus, forensic and clinical contexts have different aims, purposes, and views of these phenomena.

ABOUT THIS BOOK

Whether the issue is one of evaluating an adolescent in a court proceeding, determining the validity of a complaint of physical or psychological impairment, assessing the validity of a particular allegation or claim, or dealing with denial and resistance in mental health treatment, the need to have valid and practical methods for evaluating deceptive processes is very great. This book will focus on adolescents and their capacity to malinger or in other ways distort their self-presentation. For purposes of this discussion and those that follow, adolescence is given the qualified definition of the "teenage years," ages 13 to 19. However, this definition has its weaknesses (Coleman, 1992). There are many factors that can be used to define adolescence other than chronological age, including biological/developmental (e.g., onset of puberty), social (e.g., period of time living in parental home), and other confounding factors. The definition of adolescence as the teenage years from 13 to 19 is adopted because many of the assessment techniques discussed in this text are limited by explicit age-referenced norms.

To accomplish the task of providing practitioners with strategies for assessing malingering and deception, this book will proceed through a series of stages. In chapter 2, I will discuss specific definitions and theoretical models to provide the reader with various approaches to understanding malingering and deception. The next two chapters provide a review of assessment strategies and techniques that have applicability to the assessment process. Chapter 3 focuses on approaches to clinical interviewing, including the use of both traditional clinical interview and structured interviews that have direct relevance to malingering and deception. The use of standard adolescent psychological tests such as the MMPI–A, Millon Adolescent Clinical Inventory, Rorschach, as well as various neuropsychological tests is reviewed in chapter 4.

Of no small importance is the need for practitioners to have some sensitivity to the ethical and legal issues involved in the settings in which they practice. Therefore, chapter 5 provides an overview of ethical issues in diagnosing malingering and standards for admissibility when providing expert testimony in legal settings. Finally, the last two chapters provide examples of how the assessment of malingering and deception occurs in applied settings. Specifically, chapter 6 examines the assessment of deception in clinical and treatment-oriented situations, with a discussion of the implications that deceptive processes have for treatment planning. Chapter 7 provides a review of forensic matters that involve issues of credibility assessment, such as the voluntariness of adolescent confessions, transfer to adult status, and the evaluation of adolescents in juvenile delinquency proceedings. Throughout the text, efforts are made to provide an appropriate blend of empirical research findings and clinical case material.

CONCLUSION

The accurate assessment of deceptive forms of behavior is no easy task. There are several factors that go into evaluating these challenging phenomena, such as the motivation and intent of the individual, the context in which the behavior occurs, the developmental level of the individual, and the social pressures that influence the person's actions. Although it is not possible to know with complete certainty whether or not an individual is lying, mental health professionals are being asked with greater frequency to provide consultation or treatment in settings where the reliability and validity of adolescent self-reports are of particular concern. The need for empirically based yet practical methods for evaluating the veracity of adolescent self-reports is a prominent professional concern. This book attempts to provide practitioners with methods for conducting these evaluations in a professionally ethical and responsible fashion with the most current techniques available.

Finally, adolescence is a developmental period marked by behavioral inconsistency, oppositionality, erratic moods or behavior, and periodic disruptions in the teenager's stability. Such instability is generally taken to be a "normal" or typical defining feature of adolescence. Thus, discrepant self-reports and uncooperativeness, which are factors to be considered in the *DSM–IV* model of malingering, lack adequate specificity when they are applied to adolescents. Any clinician who has had contact with adolescents will be able to recognize that teenagers frequently make self-observations that are at odds with the clinician's assessment or "objective" findings. Moreover, adolescents are notoriously uncooperative with diagnostic evaluations and prescribed treatments to some degree. Given the very high base rate of these behaviors in adolescents, their presence in any evaluation is not likely to prove useful in distinguishing potential malingerers from honest or genuine self-reporting adolescents.

Thus, the *DSM–IV* model of malingering is puritanical, as Rogers (1990b) has observed. The model is also poorly conceived as a potential guide for diagnosing dissimulation and malingering in adolescents because many of the model's shortcomings are greatly pronounced when addressing issues arising in the psychological evaluation of adolescents.

The Pathogenic Model

According to some clinicians and researchers, malingering represents an inadequate, low-level defense process that is an individual's attempt to avoid impending decompensation or psychiatric illness. Hay (1983) has provided six case examples of individuals who feigned symptoms of schizophrenia and later developed active psychosis. Hay viewed the simulation of schizophrenia as a prodromal symptom of true psychosis. In a similar manner, Pope, Jonas, and Jones (1982) examined the outcomes of psychiatric patients exhibiting factitious psychosis. The sample consisted of patients whose psychotic symptoms were deemed to be under voluntary control for the purpose of assuming the role of a patient. All patients were assessed as having severe personality disorders and had extremely poor long-term outcomes. Extending research on this model to adolescents, Greenfeld (1987) reported the case of a 14-year-old girl who was diagnosed as feigning psychosis as part of a more severe, decompensated condition. In particular, it was noted that "feigned mental illness may now represent one of a limited number of strategies available to impoverished adolescents who otherwise cannot find a safe environment" (pp. 74–75). Indeed, some have suggested that malingering should not be diagnosed in adolescents because it invariably represents a symptom of more severe underlying psychopathology (Greenfeld, 1987; Nemzer, 1991).

This view of malingering has been referred to by Rogers (1990a) as the pathogenic model. Its hallmark is that it defines malingering and other forms of dissimulation as "ineffectual attempt[s] to control psychotic and neurotic processes by consciously reproducing underlying psychopathology" (Rogers, 1990a, pp. 323–324). Among the more damaging criticisms of the pathogenic model made by Rogers is that many malingerers do not evidence decompensation as would be predicted by the model. Also, research support for the model is based on data from inadequate sample sizes comprising only a few case studies, which were not evaluated with strict, unbiased diagnostic techniques.

Rogers (1990a) made clear that there are a few cases in which malingering represents an ineffective defensive process that precedes more active forms of psychopathology. In particular, there is the case of borderline personality disorder in which factitious symptomatology generally precipitates further decompensation and deterioration (Cunnien, 1988; Rogers, Bagby, & Rector, 1989). Given the increased attention to borderline personality disturbances in adolescence (cf. Kernberg, 1984; Masterson, 1985), it is likely that some cases of malingering and factitious presentation in adolescence can be adequately explained by the pathogenic model. However, there are still numerous instances in which adolescents will dissimulate, feign, or malinger and never fully develop more severe forms of deterioration as predicted by the model. Thus, the pathogenic model remains an inadequate framework for understanding malingering and dissimulation in adolescents.

The Adaptational Model

As described by Rogers (1990a, 1990b; Rogers, Bagby, & Dickens, 1992), the adaptational model of malingering is based on decision theory in which a given individual will malinger if doing so will result in a pos-

lescents. The detection model serves as a useful framework for conceptualizing and interpreting many of these adolescent assessment techniques.

Rogers' Proposed Classificatory Model

In response to inherent weaknesses in the *DSM* model of malingering and limitations imposed by the pathogenic model, Rogers (1990a) has formulated a proposal for classifying malingering that contains elements of the adaptational and detection models and is based on research methodology seeking to cross-validate characteristics found among malingerers with multimethod assessment procedures. The classificatory model developed by Rogers is presented in Exhibit 2.3 and represents a framework to be used in the chapters that follow. According to the organizational framework of the classificatory model, the first step in assessing for the presence of feigning is to examine the nature of a patient's self-reports. Based on a survey of empirical findings (Rogers, 1990a; Rogers et al., 1992), four basic types of self-reported symptoms have been consistently found among those who feign pathology: rare symptoms, indiscriminate reporting, blatant symptoms, and improbable symptoms.

Rare symptoms refer to those attitudes, problems, and self-reported symptoms that are very infrequent among psychiatric patients. Psychological test items or interview questions reflect highly unusual symptoms (e.g., "Do you find that listening to loud music causes painful ringing that bounces back and forth between each of your ears?"). In the classificatory model, it is taken to be a sign of malingering when an unusually high number of rare symptoms are endorsed. It is important to note that the terminology used in this model (i.e., *unusually high number*) is due to the lack of empirically established numerical cutoffs for establishing the presence or absence of malingering.

Indiscriminate symptom endorsement is another self-report style associated with malingering that is part of the classificatory model in Exhibit 2.3. This criterion comes from the observation that malingerers adopt a decision-making strategy that the more symptoms to which they admit, the more likely it is that they will be assessed as disturbed.

Exhibit 2.3

Rogers' Proposed Model for the Classification of Malingering

I. A pattern of self-reported symptoms which would include at least one of the following:

    A. Endorsement of an unusually high number of **rare symptoms** (i.e., symptoms which are very infrequent in bona fide patients).

    B. Endorsement of an unusually high number of **blatant symptoms** (i.e., symptoms which are immediately recognizable by nonprofessionals as indicative of severe psychopathology). It is often useful to ask about symptoms which are not obvious signs of mental illness (e.g., early morning awakening) for the purposes of comparison.

    C. **Nonselective endorsement of symptoms** which appear to be improbable based on the sheer number.

    D. Endorsement of **absurd and preposterous symptoms.** This criterion should be applied only to individuals who appear coherent and relevant in their speech, since some grossly psychotic patients may also endorse absurd responses.

II. Corroboration of dissimulation through one or more of the following:

    A. **Collateral interviews** which suggest that the individuals self-report is strongly indicative of feigning (e.g., family provides evidence of relatively good adjustment in contrast to self-described "gross impairment").

    B. Pronounced **differences between reported prior episodes and their clinical documentation.** Differences should be dramatic and strongly suggestive of feigning (e.g., claims of multiple suicide attempts requiring medical interventions while hospitalized, when there is no evidence in the clinical record of any suicidal ideation or gestures).

    C. Unequivocal evidence of feigning on **standardized measures** such as the MMPI and the SIRS.

Exhibit continues

Exhibit 2.3 (*Continued*)

III. Evidence based on self-report or collateral interviews that the individual's motivation for feigning was not exclusively a desire to be a patient or an attention-getting device in a borderline patient.

From Rogers et al., 1992 (p. 4). Reproduced by special permission of the Publisher, Psychological Assessment Resources, Inc., Odessa, Florida 33556, from the *Structured Interview of Reported Symptoms* by Richard Rogers, PhD, Copyright 1986, by PAR, Inc. Further reproduction is prohibited without permission of PAR, Inc.

For example, malingerers will frequently endorse a significantly higher percentage of critical items on the MMPI or will score higher on Scale F, which is a measure of infrequently reported symptoms (Greene, 1988). In short, malingerers have higher levels of self-disclosure, as measured by the sheer number of symptoms reported, than do actual patients.

The third characteristic of self-reporting found in malingerers is a high frequency of blatant symptoms endorsed. A significant number of psychological symptoms appear to be rather clear and obvious symptoms of psychopathology (e.g., hearing voices, delusions of thought insertion, suicidal ideation or intent). Support for this criterion comes from research on objective personality inventories and clinical case studies (Green, 1988; Rogers, 1984).

The fourth self-report style in malingerers is the endorsement of improbable or absurd symptoms. What distinguishes these symptoms from those that are blatant and rare is the fact that improbable symptoms are almost never reported in even the more genuinely disturbed patients, whereas malingerers will often claim their presence (e.g., "Do you often notice that your head sometimes falls off and that you have to reattach it?").

According to Rogers (1990a), the proposed classificatory model contains these four types of self-reported symptoms because they have been the ones most clearly established by empirical research to be associated with malingerers. However, Rogers also noted that other deceptive and unusual self-report strategies are worthy of further consideration and investigation. These include unusual or rare symptom combinations (e.g., feeling suicidal at the same time that the teenager has more interest in socializing with peers), increased symptom severity, and rapid onset and resolution of symptomatology. Although these strategies require further empirical exploration in adolescent populations, they provide useful criteria that should be explored in clinical and forensic evaluations.

The classificatory model outlined above is tentative in some respects; however, it has distinct advantages over other models of malingering. It is logically coherent and internally consistent, allows for the empirical testing of hypotheses, and calls for a multimethod assessment strategy for assessing and evaluating malingering and deception in adolescents. The model in Exhibit 2.3 also requires that hypotheses about a subject's self-reports be corroborated through collateral interviews, direct observation of the teenager, and reliance on objective assessment strategies and instruments. One particular aspect of adolescent dissimulation that is not covered in the classificatory model is the nature of various contextual factors that impact the consistency, veracity, and accuracy of adolescent self-reports. The next section outlines these contextual factors that can assist in applying the classificatory framework to clinical and forensic evaluations.

THE CONTEXT OF HONESTY AND DECEPTION IN ADOLESCENT SELF-REPORTS

As a stage of psychological development, adolescence is characterized by unique challenges that distinguish it from childhood and adulthood. There are demands for greater autonomy and independence brought on by closer allegiances to peer groups and a shunning of parental values and influences. Likewise, the financial and emotional ties to parents and siblings make it difficult for teenagers to pull away, rendering them prone to familial pressures and influences. Such conflict and ambivalence make for turbulence in many areas of a teenager's life.

Because of the unique challenges this developmental phase has, it follows that psychological processes will be characterized differently, depending on one's stage of development. The phenomena of malingering and other forms of deception are no different. An example will help to clarify this point. An adult who has a lengthy history of psychopathic personality characteristics and who is facing a long prison sentence will undoubtedly have some motivation to feign insanity in an attempt to avoid a long and harsh incarceration. This person may be motivated by a need to "beat the system" so as to avoid prison. Time spent in a mental hospital seems less difficult than being sent to prison, particularly if the individual has prior experiences with incarceration. A period in a mental institution is seen as "easier time." However, a juvenile may be motivated by different factors. Exhibiting signs of mental illness may be met with derision, scorn, or harassment from teenage peers in a detention center; thus, deception takes the form of minimizing psychopathology when there is an actual illness or condition that may warrant treatment.

There are internal–psychological factors that render an individual more or less likely to exhibit one form of deception over another. Also, there are external–systemic factors distinguishing the adult and juvenile justice systems from one another that may influence whether or not an individual is prone to malinger, deny, or in some other way distort their concerns. It is extremely important when assessing issues related to malingering and deception in juveniles to be aware of both internal–psychological and external–systemic factors that can play an influential role.

Contextual factors that are likely to have an impact on the veracity of adolescent self-reports are outlined in Exhibit 2.4. In particular, various factors are outlined that increase the likelihood of distortion in self-reports, including denial and malingering or feigning of mental or physical illness. These factors are divided into two types: *internal– psychological* and *external–contextual*. As noted earlier, internal– psychological factors are those pressures and influences arising from within the adolescent and representing his or her interpretation of various environmental situations or factors. These factors are mediated by the specific affective, behavioral, cognitive, and dynamic processes op-

Exhibit 2.4

Factors Contributing to Distortions in Adolescent Self-Reports

I. Increased likelihood of denial
   A. Internal–psychological factors
      1. Psychopathology not consistent with adolescent's perception of self
      2. Personality traits associated with denial or resistance
   B. External–contextual factors
      1. Greater reactivity to and concern with negative peer reactions to psychopathology
      2. Greater rehabilitative as opposed to punishment-oriented focus in juvenile system increases need to be viewed as "healthy" to avoid placement
      3. Parental influence to keep personal matters "private"
      4. Criminal or antisocial behavior viewed as a "badge of honor" by peers
      5. Denying in order to appear capable of being rehabilitated to avoid transfer from juvenile to adult court
II. Increased likelihood of malingering or feigning
   A. Internal–psychological factors
      1. "Cry for help" due to poorly developed help-seeking behavior
      2. Personality traits associated with complaining or manipulation
      3. Shorter treatment or legal history (due to age) contributes to less "sophisticated" or "informed" dissimulation
   B. External–contextual factors
      1. Feigning in order to appear mentally disordered and avoid transfer from juvenile to adult court
      2. Factitious disturbance by proxy (family dynamics)
      3. "Symptom sharing" with other disturbed adolescents
III. Other relevant factors
   A. Age of onset for many serious mental disturbances is typically in early or middle adulthood, not adolescence

Exhibit continues

Exhibit 2.4 (*Continued*)

B. Parental manipulation and influences (e.g., child custody disputes)

C. Peer group influences (e.g., gang culture)

---

erating in a given adolescent. The external–contextual factors are those creating pressures on the adolescent to behave or conform to a specific mode of conduct.

Denial and Defensiveness

There are internal–psychological factors that increase the likelihood of denial in adolescents. If symptoms of psychological disturbance are at odds with a teenager's positive self-image, such as in a narcissistic adolescent, then there is a greater likelihood of denial. Likewise, adolescents who have personality traits associated with resistance or denial, such as oppositionality, paranoia, or obsessive–compulsive tendencies, would be expected to show greater levels of denial or minimization during evaluation.

An increased chance of denial of problems or symptoms can also be expected for many adolescents because of their greater sensitivity to the reactions of peers. Adolescents are very much oriented toward acting in a way that gains favorable attention and evaluation from peers. In fact, research demonstrates that adolescents who associate with antisocial peers are at increased risk for engaging in antisocial and aggressive behavior because of peer group norms that view antisocial behavior as acceptable (Tolan, Guerra, & Kendall, 1995a). Rejection or scorn from peers is expected by many adolescents who display symptoms of severe psychopathology, particularly if the symptoms are associated with severe thought disturbances such as hallucinations, delusions, or social withdrawal. For some teenagers, symptoms of severe conduct disturbance can be held out in some peer groups as something to be admired or respected. For example, the case of Nick, a 14-year-old juvenile who was evaluated as part of disposition planning at a group home where he was placed, illustrates how conduct disturbances in adolescents can be influenced by peer-group pressures.

Nick had a history of numerous arrests over a period of one year, with charges stemming from assault, burglary, and robbery. After each offense, he appeared before a family court judge and was placed in increasingly more restrictive settings (i.e., from strict behavioral limits at home, to probation, to group home placements, and finally to a semisecure juvenile facility). Within a month after each court appearance, Nick would act out and continue to do so until he was placed in a medium-secure facility. When examined, Nick denied the severity of his actions, instead viewing them as necessary to maintain the "respect" he felt he deserved from peers in his neighborhood. "My boys understand me," he said, "so I don't care what other people think about me." To him, offending became a way to demonstrate to his peers that no police officer, judge, probation officer, or anyone in authority for that matter, was going to control his life. His offending and legal troubles served to heighten his status, in his view, among others in the neighborhood. Consequently, he minimized his personal troubles and exhibited excessive denial during the interview.

Social pressures also implicate another factor that defines the period of adolescence and contributes to the increased likelihood of denial. That is, adolescents are often more resistant and uncooperative because they are prone to see age differences between themselves and an adult examiner as increasing the likelihood that adults will fail to understand the true nature of their problems.

In conducting examinations on adolescents who are involved with the criminal justice system, it never appears to be lost on most juveniles that the "system" is more likely to treat them as in need of therapeutic services. Because the juvenile offender seeks the least restrictive placement alternative (i.e., invariably returning home with "probation" or "counseling"), they are often highly motivated to have their illegal behavior viewed as an anomaly that is outside the bounds of their regular behavioral repertoire. Mental health professionals are often called upon to assess juvenile offenders as part of the sentencing and placement phase of juvenile cases. The adolescent usually reasons that if the examiner can be convinced of his or her psychological stability, then there is less chance of being seen as requiring "treatment" or placement and the court will look more favorably on the option of returning the teenager home.

Another contextual factor that contributes to the likelihood a juvenile will deny or minimize problem areas is parental influences. In some contexts, such as child custody evaluations (Ash & Guyer, 1991), the teenager's parent may create added pressures on him or her to keep family problems concealed or private. Moreover, some less common situations may involve bizarre family customs, rituals, or dynamics that are part of a broader pathological system. Thus, parents can have both direct and indirect influences on a teenager's willingness to disclose certain problem areas. These external factors lead to greater denial and minimization during the therapeutic or evaluation interview.

Malingering and Feigning

Several additional factors have an impact on whether or not the adolescent is prone to malinger, feign, or exaggerate psychopathology. Some teenagers are not sophisticated in their ability to communicate their affective states, thus rendering them prone to exhibiting impulsive and overwhelming outbursts of emotion. That is, because some adolescents are either unwilling or unable to seek social supports and guidance, they do so in poorly planned ways. As noted in Exhibit 2.4, inadequate help-seeking behavior on the part of adolescents sometimes leads to exaggerated reports of physical or psychological problems representing an unsophisticated "cry for help." Thus, for example, a suicide threat or gesture, defiant periods of extreme oppositional behavior, or false claims of sexual abuse may reflect a plea for more parental attention and concern or represent an attempt at escaping an unbearable family situation. Likewise, certain personality propensities associated with manipulation (e.g., antisocial tendencies) or excessive complaining (e.g., avoidant, self-defeating tendencies) also raise the possibility that an adolescent may overreport or exaggerate symptomatology.

The adolescent's ideas or beliefs about mental disturbances can thus be an important contextual factor to be assessed during an examination where dissimulation is suspected. Most adolescents do not have as much experience with the mental health system or criminal justice system as do many adults with more chronic forms of psychopathology. Although some teenagers are well entrenched in these systems, there is still a relatively brief amount of time that encompasses the history of an adolescent's involvement in long-term mental health treatment. An alternative way of viewing this phenomenon is that although the history may be relatively brief (e.g., several months or a few years), it still represents a substantial proportion of the adolescent's life and is thus very significant. Over time, however, systemic factors come to play an important role in shaping the individual's self-image, behavioral repertoire, and other components of personality. The more contact or involvement one has with the mental health or criminal justice system, the more knowledgeable he or she becomes about the questions clinicians ask in their assessments, the various treatment options available, and other aspects of these systems. Thus, some individuals become "informed" and can have some knowledge about how to dissimulate in a more realistic, believable way. Because adolescents are not likely to have extensive (i.e., several years') involvement with the mental health or correctional system, their knowledge of how to present certain forms of psychopathology is likely to come from sources other than their own personal experiences. Some beliefs or ideas about symptomatology may come from the portrayal of mental disturbances in popular media, peer groups, or other sources.

Earlier I noted that juveniles may be more prone to deny or minimize pathology in order to be placed in a less restrictive setting because they do not see themselves as requiring treatment. At times, juveniles commit particularly serious criminal offenses that are seen by prosecutors as so egregious that they believe the interests of justice are best served by transferring the offenders from juvenile court and prosecuting them in adult court. In some states, it may be an adolescent's intent to appear more mentally disturbed in order to avoid transfer, whereas in other states, it may be in the teenager's perceived best interest to appear healthy to convince the court that he or she can be "rehabilitated" before a particular age. By staying in the juvenile justice system, the teenager is more likely to receive therapeutic—as opposed to punitive or correctional—interventions and services. Thus, there may be greater incentive to dissimulate in criminal cases involving transfer to adult status.

For example, the case of *United States v. Dennison* (1986) described a 16-year-old boy with a history of juvenile delinquency who was accused of stabbing to death a 20-year-old man. Although the prosecuting attorney moved to have the juvenile transferred to adult status to stand trial, the defense offered testimony from a psychologist who evaluated the juvenile's psychological functioning and treatment needs. The psychologist found that the defendant exhibited many serious symptoms of psychopathology that required inpatient treatment. Because the juvenile had no prior treatment, the psychologist concluded that there was potential for the defendant to benefit from inpatient treatment. The court agreed and ruled that the interests of justice would be best served by maintaining the defendant in juvenile court rather than transferring him to adult status.

What *Dennison* illustrated is the need to be aware of systemic factors that may impact a juvenile's clinical presentation. In that case, the 16-year-old appeared to have genuine psychopathology that required treatment, and this fact was taken into consideration by the court. However, there may be instances in which a juvenile defendant, by feigning mental illness, can avoid transfer to adult court and remain in the more rehabilitation-oriented juvenile system. By remaining in the juvenile system, there are additional advantages for the teenager, including the sealing of records when the adolescent achieves legal age and placement in less restrictive, treatment-oriented programs. Thus, when an issue is raised as to the teenager's suitability for classification as an adult offender, the issue of feigned psychopathology must be considered. However, this issue can cut both ways because it may also be the adolescent's intent to deny or minimize psychopathology to convince the examiner of one's psychological "health" or adaptability as a way of feigning potential for rehabilitation.

Clinicians who work with adolescents in inpatient units often encounter another phenomenon that reveals how setting or context can impact symptom presentation. At times, adolescents with no documented history of severe psychopathology, when placed in close proximity to, or exposed to the influence of, adolescents who experience psychiatric problems, may become more prone to "share" such symptoms as hallucinations, delusions, or severe mood disruptions. The highly publicized suicide of Nirvana rock-and-roll star Kurt Cobain prompted numerous adolescents to become "depressed" and "suicidal," adopting a presentation similar to what Millon and Davis (1996) have termed the "voguish" depressive personality disorder subtype. Such individuals philosophize about the existential emptiness and despair they feel, which gives them a feeling of belonging with others who share similar beliefs and attitudes. The clinical presentation of so-called symptom sharers, as noted in Exhibit 2.4, is that their problem seems to be driven largely by the need to belong and fit in with peers who share similar problems.

The case of Jessica, a 15-year-old White girl who was admitted for suicidal ideation, is an example. She had no prior psychiatric history, was described as a rather bright and cheerful, yet stubborn child who suddenly became suicidal shortly after the death of Kurt Cobain. She and a group of her friends began talking about the "pointlessness" of life and how empty they all felt because the rock star "really spoke to us . . . there was meaning in his message . . . now that's gone." Many of the treatment issues dealt with the confining way that her overly strict parents attempted to control her life. Addressing these issues successfully deflected Jessica from focusing on the depressive "emptiness" she shared with her friends, and she was able to deal with significant family conflict in therapy as an outpatient.

Other Contextual Factors

There are several other contextual factors that have a potential impact on the veracity and accuracy of adolescent self-reports. A few are listed in Exhibit 2.4 under the heading Other Relevant Factors. Although this brief list is not exhaustive and clearly does not reflect all potential contextual issues, it provides some insight into the various areas that can shape an adolescent's self-reports, and the factors listed are worthy of exploration in an assessment. As an example, Mikkelsen et al. (1992)

found that false allegations of sexual abuse by children and adolescents can arise within the context of a child custody evaluation when one parent consciously manipulates the child in order to gain custody. These researchers noted further that other false allegations of abuse occur in response to conscious efforts to manipulate on the part of the adolescent. Thus, many contextual factors have a direct impact on the interpretation of reports of sexual abuse.

Another relevant factor to be considered when evaluating adolescent reports of psychopathology is the different age of onset for specific forms of serious mental disturbances. When feigned psychosis or affective disorder is suspected, clinicians recognize that the more serious illnesses such as schizophrenia have their onset, though not invariably, in early adulthood. However, such factors cannot be controlling in the clinician's decision-making process, because some adolescents do in fact suffer from serious mental illnesses. Consideration of typical age of onset is important in evaluating the adolescent because it can provide mild corroborating, but not definitive, evidence of dissimulation. Only when other data obtained from psychological testing, clinical interviews, history, and collateral reports are suggestive of feigning can age of onset become an additional factor in the decision-making equation.

CONCLUSION

This chapter reviewed the various definitions of specific terms used to classify various types of self-reports, ranging from honest to dissimulated responding. There are a number of self-report styles, including denial and honest, irrelevant, and dissimulated reporting, with denial and malingering as the two major types of deceptive self-report styles. In addition, several models for conceptualizing malingering and deception were reviewed, including the *DSM–IV*, pathogenic, adaptational, detection, and Rogers' classificatory models.

As I reviewed the research and scientific literature during preparation of this text, it became clear that research on malingering and deception focuses almost entirely on adults and very little on adolescents. The once-held belief that adolescents are merely "mini-adults" has long been shed in favor of more age-appropriate models for understanding the behavior of adolescents and age-normed assessment techniques for measuring and quantifying phenomena in this age group. Based on the literature reviewed in this chapter, it should be clear that current models for conceptualizing malingering and dissimulation, particularly the *DSM–IV* and pathogenic models, are inadequate for diagnosing deceptive processes in adolescence. Although the classificatory model proposed by Rogers, based in part on detection and adaptational approaches, holds the most promise, it has not been adequately tested in adolescent populations. Moreover, I have reviewed various contextual factors that impact the accuracy and veracity of adolescent self-reports, and I argue here that such factors must be a part of any comprehensive assessment of feigning or deceptive processes in adolescents.

Given the current status of understanding adolescent deception, adequate assessment must invariably rest on the use of clinical assessment strategies that are guided and informed by empirical research. As Rogers (1988b) stated, "The strength of clinical assessment in the evaluation of malingering and defensiveness remains chiefly in the use of well-validated individual measures. The synthesis of these measures is, with few exceptions, more an art of clinical judgment than an empirically based process" (p. 306). Future research will undoubtedly expand the understanding of how and why adolescents feign or deny problems and pathology. However, thorough and diligent clinical practice requires that conclusions be reasonable and justified based on data obtained from reliable and valid sources. In the next two chapters, I will review various interviewing strategies and techniques and psychological testing approaches to help guide clinical and forensic evaluations on this important issue.

3

Interviewing Techniques and Strategies

The standard method for collecting information and conducting clinical evaluations in mental health settings has traditionally been the clinical interview. In its most basic form, a clinical interview represents a "deliberately initiated conversation wherein two persons . . . engage in *verbal and nonverbal* communication toward the end of gathering information which will help one or both parties better reach a goal" (Matarazzo, 1978, p. 47; emphasis added). One key component of this definition is that the interview consists of not only verbal questions and responses but also nonverbal forms of communication. In the assessment of malingering, defensiveness, and other types of deception, the clinician not only formulates questions and makes note of the responses but also analyzes nonverbal communication during the interview. Such factors as consistency of the adolescent's responses, specificity or vagueness when responding, and other similar qualities in response style are paralinguistic, stylistic aspects to conversations that must be noted. The clinical interview affords opportunities to collect information that cannot be found anywhere else in the evaluation process. As Nuttall and Ivey (1986) have noted, the diagnostic interview with adolescents allows for flexibility in the questions and probes used to elicit information, the evaluation of subjective experiences on the part of the adolescent, more personal contact that can foster either more open or restricted communication by the adolescent, the chance to observe nonverbal behavior, and the opportunity to collect historical data.

Given the fact that forensic evaluation procedures are often subjected to scrutiny and often need to be defended in courtroom settings, the interview may often be attacked on the grounds that it lacks standardization, that it has poor reliability or consistency across different interviews, and that clinicians who conduct the interview often hold biases against the interviewee. Therefore, any procedures that help to organize and standardize the interview process will lead to more coherent testimony and legally defensible techniques when using the interview for forensic evaluations and for more accurate diagnosis and appropriate treatment planning in clinical assessments. Even in clinical settings, standardized interviewing procedures can assume broader coverage of clinical symptomatology that can assist with appropriate treatment planning. Although some may argue that standardized interviewing procedures interfere with the "flow" of psychotherapy, the more information a clinician has available, the more likely it is that treatment will be appropriately structured.

There are various methods for standardizing the clinical evaluation process. One method, which is the focus of the next chapter, is standardized psychological testing procedures. The second method, the focus of this chapter, is standard clinical interview techniques. Structured interviews are instruments that have been used in recent years to aid in the standardization of clinical diagnostic interviewing. Instruments such as the Diagnostic Interview Schedule (DIS; Robins, Helzer, Cottler, & Goldring, 1989), Schedule of Affective Disorders and Schizophrenia (SADS; Spitzer & Endicott, 1978), and Structured Clinical Interview for *DSM−III−R* Disorders (SCID; Spitzer, Williams, Gibbon, & First, 1990a, 1990b) are examples of structured interviews. According to Rogers (1995), structured interviews outline a standard format for both questions and answers, provide thorough coverage of symptomatology for particular diagnostic categories, aid in the determination of indiscriminant responding, and allow clinicians to assess consistency in self-reports. Another method for standardizing the clinical interview is a variant of structured interviews, often called semistructured interviews. Although not formally published in the manner that structured interview schedules are, semistructured interviews represent adaptations of organized material such as diagnostic categories or adaptations of structured interviews in a form that allows for greater flexibility.

In this chapter, I will review structured interview techniques for assessing malingering and deception in adolescents. Because adolescent malingering has not been the focus of much research, there are no structured interviews that have been designed specifically for assessing malingering in adolescents. The only instrument designed for malingering and deception is the Structured Interview of Reported Symptoms (SIRS; Rogers, Bagby, & Dickens, 1992). Therefore, I will review this instrument in terms of its psychometric properties, including its reliability and validity as a measure of feigning and dissimulation. Its use in adolescent populations will also be reviewed. Then, I will examine other general structured interviews with respect to their applications in assessing the veracity of adolescent self-reports. Following this discussion there is an overview of various semistructured and clinical interviewing strategies that are helpful in assessing adolescent malingering and deception.

STRUCTURED INTERVIEWS

Structured interviews constitute reliable methods for obtaining comprehensive diagnostic information. Moreover, they reduce the negative effects of information variance in which different interviews provide different pieces of information that can impact the resultant conclusions and diagnoses (Rogers, 1995). That is, they help to assure that two different interviewers, examining the same person, will ask similar questions and explore similar symptom clusters. By employing common standards for asking questions and scoring patient responses, there is a reduction in the inconsistency that can arise from various question formats. Moreover, there is a greater likelihood that important areas of inquiry will not be overlooked when structured interviews are used.

These procedures are not without their drawbacks, however. Excessive reliance on structured interviews can lead to routinized, rapport-inhibiting interactions with interviewees, and the potential for misdiagnosis due to lack of comprehensiveness in coverage is a concern (Rogers, 1995). Nevertheless, they can and should be an important source of information in clinical and forensic evaluations.

Of the structured interviews available, a few have potential use in the assessment of malingering and deception in juveniles. Two specific instruments that are particularly useful include the Structured Interview of Reported Symptoms (SIRS) and the Psychopathy Checklist–Revised (PCL–R). After discussion of these two specific instruments and a short review of others, some general structured interview techniques will be briefly reviewed.

Structured Interview of Reported Symptoms (SIRS)

The SIRS is a 172-item structured interview booklet that is designed to assess a wide range of symptoms of psychopathology. There are eight primary scales and five supplementary scales that are designed to measure feigning and defensiveness. More important, the content of items and scales on the SIRS has been varied in order to prevent the instrument from being perceived as a measure of feigning for any particular mental disorder. That is, the SIRS is intended to be a generalized measure of feigning, regardless of the specific mental disorder being assessed.

Questions are divided into two alternate sets of the scales that are combined to form the complete instrument. Thus, there are six sections in the SIRS: Detailed Inquiries I, General Inquiries I, Repeated Inquiries I, Detailed Inquiries II, General Inquiries II, and Repeated Inquiries II. Exhibit 3.1 outlines the eight primary and five supplementary scales that make up the SIRS profile. Each primary scale is scored and plotted on a profile that has four graded classifications to aid in interpretation: Honest Responding, Indeterminate, Probable Feigning, and Definite Feigning.

The SIRS is designed to measure various self-report tendencies associated with feigning and distortion that are found in Rogers' classi-

Exhibit 3.1

Description of the SIRS Scales

I. Primary scales

    A. **Rare Symptoms (RS)** measures genuine symptoms that arise infrequently in psychiatric patients.

    B. **Symptom Combination (SC)** measures the pairing of genuine symptoms that rarely occur together.

    C. **Improbable or Absurd Symptoms (IA)** measures symptoms that are preposterous or highly unlikely to occur in actual patient populations.

    D. **Blatant Symptoms (BL)** measures the tendency to overendorse the number of obvious signs of mental disorder.

    E. **Subtle Symptoms (SU)** measures the tendency to overendorse everyday problems and symptoms that are not always associated with mental illness.

    F. **Severity of Symptoms (SEV)** measures the tendency to rate the severity of symptoms experienced as extreme or unbearable.

    G. **Selectivity of Symptoms (SEL)** measures indiscriminate and nonselective endorsement of psychiatric symptoms.

    H. **Reported versus Observed Symptoms (RO)** assesses discrepancies between what the patient states is problematic and what is actually observed by focusing on overt speech and physical movements.

II. Supplementary scales

    A. **Direct Appraisal of Honesty (DA)** measures direct perceptions about one's *honesty, truthfulness, and completeness* of self-reports.

    B. **Defensive Symptoms (DS)** measures the patient's tendency to deny or minimize a variety of common everyday problems and worries that most people experience from time to time.

    C. **Symptom Onset (SO)** assesses symptoms that have a sudden or uncharacteristically rapid onset.

Exhibit continues

Exhibit 3.1 (Continued)

Description of the SIRS Scales

D. **Overly Specified Symptoms (OS)** measures symptoms that are described with an unreasonable or unrealistic degree of specificity or precision.

E. **Inconsistency of Symptoms (INC)** a measure of unreliable or inconsistent reporting of symptoms.

---

ficatory model that was outlined in chapter 2. Each SIRS question represents a highly specific and detailed inquiry into either a specific symptom or an observation about the patient's expression of particular symptoms. Given the highly structured nature of the questions, administration of the SIRS is a very straightforward, uncomplicated task. Any detailed follow-up questions are a standard part of the interview, so the administration process is objective and clear-cut, with answers assigned numerical ratings of X *(No Answer* or *Unratable),* 0 *(No),* 1 *(Qualified Yes* or *Sometimes),* and 2 *(Definite Yes).*

Because of the highly structured nature of the SIRS interview, interrater reliabilities are quite high, ranging from 0.89 to 1.00 for both the primary and supplementary scales (Rogers et al., 1992). The internal consistency (α) of the SIRS scales is also quite acceptable for the primary scales, ranging from 0.77 on Reported versus Observed Symptoms to 0.92 on Blatant Symptoms and Subtle Symptoms. Internal consistency coefficients are not appropriate for scales Severity of Symptoms, Selectivity of Symptoms, and Inconsistency of Symptoms because they are the product of summing (Rogers et al., 1992). The supplementary scales have lower internal consistency coefficients due mainly to the relatively fewer number of items composing these scales. For example, scale Symptom Onset (with only 2 items) has an alpha coefficient of 0.66, and scales Direct Appraisal of Honesty, Defensive Systems, and Overly Specified Symptoms (with 8, 19, and 7 items, respectively) have respective alpha coefficients of 0.75, 0.82, and 0.77.

These internal consistency coefficients are generally acceptable for both clinical and forensic applications. In his outline on guidelines for selecting psychological tests in forensic settings, Heilbrun (1992) recommended a reliability coefficient of 0.80 for any measure that is to be used in forensic assessments; otherwise, explicit justification for a particular test's use must be made. The primary justification for higher reliability is that validity is limited by reliability and lower reliability yields excessive error variance. On the SIRS primary scales, five out of the six scales for which reliability coefficients can be calculated exceed 0.80, showing very respectable internal consistency; the supplementary scales approach 0.80. Because the SIRS is the only structured interview designed specifically for feigning and dissimulation, its use can be clearly justified in forensic settings on these grounds, and the high interrater and internal consistency reliability can also be cited in support of its use.

Another major consideration in selecting a measure for forensic application is the test's relevance to a specific forensic psychological construct and the availability of supportive research on its relevance in validation studies (Heilbrun, 1992). There is a sound body of research supporting validity of the SIRS. Rogers, Gillis, Dickens, and Bagby (1991) found that the SIRS was excellent at differentiating a group of 40 participants who were asked to simulate a serious mental illness and 41 control participants who were asked to respond honestly. With the exception of scale Defensive Symptoms (which was not intended to be a measure of malingering), all SIRS scales successfully differentiated simulators from controls. Moreover, there was support for concurrent validity of SIRS scales in that they correlated in expected directions with MMPI validity scales and indices. Rogers and his colleagues then examined the ability of the SIRS to differentiate suspected malingerers from a sample of psychiatric inpatients with genuine psychiatric disturbances and found it was able to do so effectively.

Other studies carried out by Rogers and his colleagues have supported the robustness of the SIRS across a variety of populations and contexts. In a sample of correctional inmates, representing antisocial individuals, the instrument was able to discriminate between simulators and controls (Rogers, Gillis, & Bagby, 1990). Moreover, this study found that, contrary to widely held beliefs, antisocial individuals were not more effective malingerers than were clinical and community control samples. Another factor examined by Rogers, Gillis, Bagby, and Monteiro (1991) was the impact of participants' having general information about psychiatric disorders and techniques for minimizing detection (i.e., through coaching) on the ability of the SIRS to accurately distinguish malingerers from genuine patients. Results from this study revealed that participants coached on how to modify their clinical presentation were able to alter their scores on all SIRS scales designed to assess malingering. *However,* the SIRS was still able to correctly classify 97% of inpatients with genuine psychiatric disturbances and 85% of coached simulators. Finally, the SIRS has been found to be an effective generalized measure of feigning in that it functions well for a variety of psychiatric disorders, including schizophrenia, major depression, and anxiety disorders (Rogers, Kropp, & Bagby, 1993).

Although these studies support the validity and utility of the SIRS as a generalized measure of malingering in adults, the more crucial question remains as to whether or not this instrument has any utility in adolescent populations. As history has shown, adaptation of adult tests to adolescents can be problematic, absent validation of such measures on adolescents (Archer & Ball, 1988). In a study on the validity of various instruments to measure feigning in adolescents, Rogers, Hinds, and Sewell (1996) examined the ability of the SIRS to identify malingering in a sample of 14- to 17-year-olds. The study sample consisted of adolescents who were dually diagnosed with substance abuse disorder and at least one other diagnosis, such as dysthymia, oppositional–defiant, conduct, adjustment, and anxiety disorders. Each adolescent was administered the SIRS, MMPI–A, and Screening Index of Malingered Symptoms (SIMS) under honest conditions and then again under one of three simulated conditions in which the adolescent was given a financial incentive to feign schizophrenia, major depression, or generalized anxiety disorder after being given a brief description of the disorder and examples of representative symptoms.

This extremely important study by Rogers and his colleagues found support for the concurrent validity of the SIRS primary scales against the criterion of the F-minus-K index on the MMPI–A and scale $F(p)$, which is a newly developed measure on the MMPI–2 designed to identify malingerers (Arbisi & Ben-Porath, 1995). In addition, Rogers and colleagues found that the SIRS performed very well in identifying feigning in adolescents. Table 3.1 presents the results obtained from this study for the individual SIRS primary scales and Table 3.2 presents classification rates based on a composite SIRS profile index defined by one primary scale in the "Definite" range, or ≥ 3 (or ≥ 2) scales in the "Probable" range. An examination of Tables 3.1 and 3.2 reveals that the SIRS composite indices demonstrate excellent overall classification rates.

Because optimal cutoffs in Tables 3.1 and 3.2 were developed from the sample on which the classification rates were computed, they are vulnerable to what Rogers et al. (1996) called "overfitting the data." In other words, because the optimal cutoffs represent the "best fit" for their study's adolescent sample, they are highly prone to overestimating the actual positive and negative predictive power of these cutoffs. Additional cross-validation is necessary before these alternative cutoffs for adolescents can be adopted with confidence.

Although this study represents only one preliminary report on validity of the SIRS for adolescents, it does support the use of this instrument in the assessment of feigning in adolescents. Moreover, cutoffs established in the SIRS manual appear to be acceptable for adolescent populations. However, Rogers and his colleagues recommend what appears to be a sound approach to using the SIRS with younger subjects. Because there is a great risk in inappropriately diagnosing an adolescent as a malingerer who is, in fact, not malingering (i.e., not getting appropriate treatment), it is recommended that the SIRS be used as corroborative data. That is, SIRS results should be used to corroborate impressions derived from the history, clinical interview, and other psychometric data (see chap. 4). Additionally, to minimize the likelihood of costly false positives (i.e., bona fide patients inappropriately identified as feigners), a composite index in Table 3.2 is highly unlikely to misclassify honest self-reporters as feigners, given the high negative pre-

Table 3.1

SIRS Cutting Scores for Adolescents

SIRS scale	Established criteria[a]			Optimal criteria[b]		
	Cutoff	PPP	NPP	Cutoff	PPP	NPP
Rare Symptoms	>4	0.55	0.94	>4	0.55	0.94
Symptom Combination	>6	0.40	0.98	>4	0.51	0.98
Improbable/Absurd	>5	0.36	1.00	>2	0.55	0.98
Blatant	>10	0.60	0.98	>9	0.66	0.98
Subtle	>15	0.64	0.98	>13	0.74	0.94
Selectivity	>17	0.49	1.00	>13	0.77	0.94
Severity	>9	0.68	1.00	>7	0.75	0.94
Reported versus Observed	>6	0.59	0.96	>4	0.72	0.91

NOTE: PPP = positive predictive power; NPP = negative predictive power. (See chap. 5 in this book for a complete description of these terms.)

[a]Established criteria are based on cutting scores from the SIRS manual (Rogers, Bagby, & Dickens, 1992).
[b]Optimal criteria are cutting scores based on the adolescent sample from Rogers, Hinds, and Sewell (1996).

Table 3.2

Clinical Interpretation of SIRS for Adolescents Based on Composite Index

SIRS Composite Index[a]	Established criteria[b]		Optimal criteria[c]	
	PPP	NPP	PPP	NPP
1 Definite or ≥3 Probable	0.66	1.00	0.81	0.96
1 Definite or ≥2 Probable	0.79	0.98	0.89	0.94

[a]Composite Index identifies an individual as feigning if one SIRS scale falls in the Definite range or a given number fall in the Probable range.
[b]Established criteria are based on cutting scores from the SIRS manual (Rogers, Bagby, & Dickens, 1992).
[c]Optimal criteria are cutting scores based on the adolescent sample from Rogers, Hinds, and Sewell (1996).

dictive power values. Additional cross-validation is required to determine whether modified cutoffs are required for adolescents. Therefore, the adult norms and cutoffs outlined in the SIRS manual (Rogers et al., 1992) should be utilized when using the SIRS with adolescents.

I have used the SIRS in a substantial number of clinical and forensic evaluations involving adolescents. I have relied also on the measure primarily to corroborate findings from other instruments such as the Minnesota Multiphasic Personality Inventory–Adolescent (MMPI–A; Butcher et al., 1992) or Millon Adolescent Clinical Inventory (MACI; Millon, 1993) and data generated from clinical interviews and collateral contacts with family members. Based on this sample of adolescent cases, the SIRS appears to function well, and it requires little or no modification in administration. However, there are a few recurring questions that adolescents seem to ask during administration and there are some SIRS items that deserve careful attention. For example, item 155 on the SIRS asks the participant if he or she has observed changes in the way his or her body looks. There is a follow-up question that is asked if the participant responds in the affirmative by which the examiner explores whether or not the changes are due to growing older or physical illness. With adolescents, responses to the first question are typically, but not always, in the affirmative due to physical maturation and development related to puberty. Therefore, the follow-up question is very important to ask to make sure that the item is not scored unless changes are attributed to something other than age or physical illness. Another common problem when administering the SIRS to adolescents is that some of the questions may not be well understood by the adolescent. For example, when asked if one hears "unnatural" sounds or voices (Item 41), an adolescent may respond by asking for clarification. The best response to such queries is to simply ask the question again, *in the exact same format as the SIRS item.* A change in rate of speech, emphasis on particular words, or pausing between words has been found in my experience to be sufficient for clarifying the question and obtaining a scorable response. This initial reponse does not violate standard administration procedures because questions are not paraphrased or altered. If an adolescent continues to have difficulty understanding the question, providing a simple and brief definition of one word in the item is generally sufficient to obtain a response. If an adolescent persists in having difficulty understanding an item, then selection of the "No Answer" response on the answer sheet is recommended, thus avoiding lengthy discussions with the adolescent as to the meaning of a particular question. Experience with using the SIRS in adolescent populations suggests that the inability of adolescents to understand the items is very rare, except with resistant or cognitively limited participants.

Psychopathy Checklist–Revised (PCL–R)

The PCL–R is a structured interview developed by Hare (1980, 1991) as a measure of the personality construct of psychopathy as originally formulated by Cleckley (1976). Although the PCL–R is not designed as a measure of malingering or deception, the instrument can potentially add a significant amount of information to the assessment of deception in adolescent subjects. More specifically, the PCL–R can provide important insight into the meaning of lying or deception for a given individual by placing these behaviors within the context of the individual's personality style. In other words, the PCL–R can be useful in answering such questions as whether or not lying and deception are part of a deeply ingrained personality style that renders the adolescent highly prone to manipulate and con other people, or whether they are isolated symptoms. Other information that the PCL–R can provide is the differentiation of chronic lying that is motivated by self-centered gain and self-aggrandizement from other motivations. In short, the instrument can offer valuable information on the relationship between deception and personality.

The role of lying and deception in psychopathic character types has been outlined by Meloy (1988). A major trait of psychopathic personality is narcissism; lying and manipulation are frequently utilized to enhance the self-image and to produce grandiosity to protect the self from vulnerability. That is, psychopathic individuals attempt to intentionally manipulate and take advantage of others not only to obtain some goal but to devalue and humiliate others to promote the psychopath's self-image. Therefore, lying and deception are frequently accompanied by affective states of exhilaration and contempt when deception is successful because the victim of the deception is devalued while the psychopathic person's pride is enhanced. This form of contemptuous delight in the psychopath differs from the situationally related feeling of delight in the nonpsychopath in that psychopaths are incapable of feeling the associated guilt and remorse that overcomes the nonpsychopath's delight. This differentiation can have important implications in diagnosis and treatment planning. Thus, the presence or absence of psychopathic character pathology is an important consideration in many evaluations where deception is suspected.

The PCL–R is a 20-item checklist and as the list of PCL–R items in Exhibit 3.2 reveals, psychopathic individuals exhibit a deeply ingrained, long-standing style of functioning that has an early onset. Psychopaths are superficially charming; exhibit a grandiose sense of self-worth; and engage in a pattern of manipulative, predatory, and impulsive behavior. They show very little empathy for others, have little or no anxiety, and they lack remorse for their antisocial acting out. At least two of the PCL–R items have direct reference to lying and decep-

---

Exhibit 3.2

Psychopathy Checklist–Revised (PCL–R) Items

1. Glibness/Superficial Charm
2. Grandiose Sense of Self-Worth
3. Need for Stimulation/Proneness to Boredom
4. **Pathological Lying**
5. **Conning/Manipulative**
6. Lack of Remorse or Guilt
7. Shallow Affect
8. Callous/Lack of Empathy
9. Parasitic Lifestyle
10. Poor Behavioral Controls
11. Promiscuous Sexual Behavior
12. Early Behavior Problems
13. Lack of Realistic Long-Term Goals
14. Impulsivity
15. Irresponsibility
16. Failure to Accept Responsibility for Own Actions
17. Many Short-Term Marital Relationships
18. Juvenile Delinquency
19. Revocation of Conditional Release
20. Criminal Versatility

---

tion: Pathological Lying (Item 4) and Conning/Manipulative (Item 5). Other items have a tangential or indirect relationship to deception; for example, Parasitic Lifestyle (Item 9) implies a deceptive pattern of taking unempathically from others, and Failure to Accept Responsibility for Own Actions (Item 16) implies a degree of deception by ignoring obvious facts about one's behavior.

Administration of the PCL–R requires a substantial investment of time and effort. It is very important to recognize that the PCL–R is *not* scored after a cursory or even standard clinical interview with the subject. Proper administration of the instrument involves two steps: an interview with the patient *and* review of collateral information, including interviews with other people who have contact with the participant or review of documents and records. In all, the PCL–R takes approximately 1½ to 2 hours to complete and involves filling out a comprehensive booklet covering the participant's educational, occupational, family, marital, and criminal history. Once all of the data are collected, each PCL–R item is then scored on a three-point scale of 0 *(the item does not apply)*, 1 *(the item applies to some extent)*, or 2 *(the item is a good fit)*. Therefore, the total PCL–R score can range from a low of 0 to a high of 40.

In addition to an overall PCL–R score, the instrument provides two factor scores that are clinically useful because they have different patterns of intercorrelation with other variables (Hare et al., 1990). Table 3.3 outlines two factors that define different dimensions of psychopathy. Factor I reflects a selfish, callous, and remorseless use of others; this factor has high loadings on the two PCL–R items associated with lying and deception. Factor II is associated with a chronically unstable, antisocial, and deviant lifestyle. High scores on Factor I can be helpful in identifying interpersonal and affective personality traits that reflect a long-standing lack of concern and empathy for others, of which lying and deception may be a major characteristic.

Although the PCL–R manual outlines excellent psychometric data for adult male prison and forensic populations, there are several factors that caution against strict application of the PCL–R to adolescent populations. For example, adolescents may not have engaged in a sufficient amount of criminal or antisocial activity to meet criteria for Items 18 (Juvenile Delinquency) and 20 (Criminal Versatility). To address these concerns, Forth, Hart, and Hare (1990) created a modified 18-item version of the PCL–R, which was tested on a sample of 13- to 20-year-old male offenders. Two items were dropped (i.e., Items 9 [Parasitic Lifestyle] and 17 [Many Short-Term Marital Relationships]) because they are believed to be inappropriate for adolescents and are scored on

Table 3.3
Psychopathy Checklist–Revised (PCL–R) Factors

Factor I: Selfish, callous, and remorseless use of others	Factor II: Chronically unstable, antisocial, and socially deviant lifestyle
1. Glibness/Superficial Charm	3. Need for Stimulation/Proneness to Boredom
2. Grandiose Sense of Self-Worth	
4. **Pathological Lying**	9. Parasitic Lifestyle
5. **Conning/Manipulative**	10. Poor Behavioral Controls
6. Lack of Remorse or Guilt	12. Early Behavior Problems
7. Shallow Affect	13. Lack of Realistic Goals
8. Callous/Lack of Empathy	14. Impulsivity
16. Failure to Accept Responsibility for Own Actions	15. Irresponsibility
	18. Juvenile Delinquency
	19. Revocation of Conditional Release

NOTE: Copyright 1991 Multi-Health Systems Inc., 908 Niagara Falls Blvd., North Tonawanda, NY 14120-2060, (800) 456-3003. Reproduced by permission. Emphasis added.

the basis of work and marital histories. Also, two items (i.e., Item 18 [Juvenile Delinquency] and 20 [Criminal Versatility]) had their scoring modified to account for the shorter life of adolescents because these items are scored based on a lifelong pattern of behavior.

With this modified version of the PCL–R, Forth and colleagues established excellent reliability for the instrument at a level exceeding the 0.80 reliability coefficient standard cited by Heilbrun (1992). Inter-rater reliabilities for the overall psychopathy score ranged from 0.88 to 0.94 and internal consistency (Cronbach's α) was determined to be 0.90. Moreover, PCL–R scores correlated highly with several variables, including the number of conduct disorder symptoms present, prior violent offenses, recidivism, and institutional violence (i.e., aggressive or violent acts committed while incarcerated). These results are encouraging, but they do not provide definitive evidence of the validity of the PCL–R for adolescent assessment.

For research purposes, Hare (1991) and Forth et al. (1990) have adopted a cutoff score of 30 or more as indicative of psychopathy in adolescents. At the present time, adoption of the PCL–R in adolescent assessments awaits further cross-validation. Although an approach similar to that recommended for the SIRS may be considered (i.e., use of the instrument as *corroborative* data and not as definitive), one must still be cognizant of the implications of identifying a juvenile offender as psychopathic and the long-term effects such a determination will have on that teenager's interaction with the legal system (Forth et al., 1990).

Other Structured Interviews for Adolescents

Most structured diagnostic interviews were originally developed to assist with standardizing interview procedures in programs of research. As many of these instruments have become extensively tested in terms of their psychometric properties, they are more commonly being used in clinical assessment. Although the SIRS, and to a lesser extent the PCL–R, is useful in assessing the veracity of adolescent self-reports, other general structured interviews may have some indirect benefits and subtle advantages. In particular, the ability of these instruments to provide standardized normative data on adolescent self-reports can also allow for comparisons between a given adolescent in clinical or forensic settings and a broader normative sample. As outlined earlier, rare, unusual, or absurd symptoms are associated with feigning, as are unusual symptom combinations and indiscriminate responding. Evidence of such responding in structured interviews can be important information for the clinician.

Specific interviews that have been designed for adolescent populations include the Schedule of Affective Disorders and Schizophrenia for School-Age Children (K–SADS; Ambrosini, 1992), Diagnostic Interview Schedule for Children (DISC; National Institute of Mental Health, 1991), Children's Assessment Schedule (CAS; Hodges, McKnew, Cytryn, Stern, & Kline, 1982), and the Diagnostic Interview for Children and Adolescents–Revised–Adolescent Version (DICA–R–A; Reich, Shayka, & Taibleson, 1991a, 1991b). Rogers (1995) provided an excellent review on these stuctured interviews and reviews the reliability, validity, and clinical applications of each. According to his assessment, the K–SADS and DISC fare somewhat better than the CAS or the DICA–R–A. For a more in-depth analysis of each, the reader is referred to Rogers (1995).

For purposes of assessing malingering and deception in juveniles, both comprehensive and specialized structured interviews provide standardized diagnostic inquiries, permitting patient reponses to be compared against set diagnostic criteria and decision trees. Thus, although they may not directly assess malingering or deception, they can provide corroborative or disconfirming evidence for particular diagnoses. By comparing an adolescent's reponses on structured interviews to established criteria, the clinician can obtain data that can help confirm or rule out a diagnosis or clinical presentation that is suspected of having some degree of feigning or dissimulation as a major component.

CLINICAL INTERVIEW STRATEGIES

Clinical hunches, intuition, and other unvalidated and unsubstantiated indices have often formed the basis for many opinions in the assessment of malingering and deception. Unfortunately, there is no systematically controlled research that has examined the ability of unstructured clinical interviews to identify patients who are malingering or dissimulating (Ziskin & Faust, 1988). Because clinicians have been consistently shown to be imperfect and indeed poor in their clinical judgment and ability to predict (Dawes, 1995; Kahneman & Tversky, 1973; Wiggins, 1981), it can be concluded that clinicians who base their decisions about an individual's potential feigning or dissimulation solely on unstructured clinical interviews are basing their opinions on a methodologically flawed technique. Therefore, interviews should be combined with data from patient histories, psychological testing results, structured interviews, and clinical observations in order to make informed decisions.

Despite limitations of clinical interviews as the sole basis for making clinical decisions, they do constitute an integral part of the overall assessment. Sometimes unstructured interactions with an adolescent can offer unique insights and an opportunity for direct observations into how the teenager manages interpersonal relationships and manifests his or her pathology when given "free reign" to interact with others. At times, structured interviews and psychological testing can be restrictive of the responses available to an adolescent. That is, a balanced approach that recognizes strengths and limitations in all techniques that are used is a more appropriate stance to take when conducting assessments.

Although structured interviews such as the SIRS and PCL–R hold several advantages in their assessment of malingering and deception in juveniles, research on these techniques with adolescent populations has been limited. In response to this state of affairs, it was noted earlier that the recommended approach to using these instruments in evaluations is to consider their results as corroborative data for confirming or disproving hypotheses derived from other parts of the evaluation. Although practitioners may often feel as though they are left with little else to rely on than a clinical interview and the occasional psychological testing results, this does not have to be the case. Clinical approaches to interviewing can involve systematic and organized approaches to taking a psychosocial history, performing a mental status examination, and collecting contextual information relevant to the questions being addressed by the assessment.

An Interviewing Framework

The clinical interview is easier to manage and is more efficient when it is organized and has a logical framework. In fact, over time, most clinicians adopt an outline, either written or mental, for conducting clinical interviews. Typically, the interview begins with preliminary issues and formalities that set the context (e.g., "Tell me what brings you here.") and progresses through taking of the psychosocial history, a formal mental status examination, additional diagnostic questions, explorations of unresolved issues, and a formal close to the interview. Interviewers generally feel more comfortable when there is a clear focus to the interview. Exhibit 3.3 provides a framework that is proposed for helping to organize material obtained from the clinical interview, along with examples of relevant factors that can be explored on interview. The examples are not exhaustive and serve only as a guideline. This

---

Exhibit 3.3

**Factors Related to Adolescent Dissimulation
in Clinical Interviews**

I. Individual factors (Rogers & Resnick, 1988)
   A. Clinical observations
      1. Inconsistency
      2. Unusual symptom combinations
   B. Self-reports
      1. Blatant
      2. Subtle
      3. Intermediate
   C. Adolescent self-perceptions of psychopathology
II. Contextual factors (see Exhibit 2.4)
   A. Familial or peer influences
   B. Popular culture
   C. Forensic/clinical setting
III. Historical factors
   A. Consistency/inconsistency between present and past presentation
   B. Prior exposure to psychopathology (e.g., prior hospitalization)
   C. Recent changes or stressors
   D. Collateral information (e.g., parents, teachers, documents, records)

---

framework is not meant to serve as a comprehensive outline for assessing malingering and deception in the clinical or forensic evaluation; rather, it serves as a method for highlighting some of the more salient factors that are to be assessed in the interview and helps to organize various aspects of the clinical examination.

The first set of factors that make up any part of a clinical interview are those oriented toward the individual. These include such things as clinical observations, patient self-reports, diagnostic presentation, and other means by which diagnosis, personality, and clinical symptomatology are evaluated from information provided by the individual. The approach to clinical interviewing that works very well with respect to the assessment of feigning and dissimulation is the one outlined by Rogers and Resnick (1988); their stated goal is to "provide a framework for mental health professionals to derive their own systematic inquiries based on their particular settings" (p. 12). Consequently, strategies for interviewing adolescents and assessing feigning can follow this general strategy, with specific modifications in the format of some questions and the types of observations made in order to conform to the special needs and concerns of adolescents. Three different levels of strategic questioning have been proposed by Rogers and Resnick (1988). These levels correspond to the degree of transparency a teenager may manifest in his or her responses, namely blatant, subtle, and intermediate symptomatology and concerns. Blatant self-reports are those that are of clear psychopathological significance (e.g., "I hear voices"). Subtle self-reports are those that reveal problems that many adolescents experience but which are not necessarily pathological (e.g., "My parents are hassling me"). Intermediate self-reports are those that are suggestive of psychopathology, but the severity is unclear at first (e.g., "My friends make fun of me"). Clinical interviewing can proceed by analyzing the relative degree to which blatant, subtle, and intermediate reports are made in the interview. In this way, the level of severity that the adolescent wishes to convey can be appraised.

In addition to these strategies, adolescents are also prone to manifest some signs of deception that clinical experience has shown are not as common in adult populations. For instance, concern that parents may learn of a particular problem and resistance to meeting in family interviews suggests a desire on the part of the adolescent to conceal certain information. Although this is an attempt to deceive the parents or the clinician, such a stance tends to arise in cases where the problems or symptoms are bona fide instead of feigned. Also, by asking the adolescent to provide self-perceptions about how he or she views the clinical symptomatology experienced, valuable insights may be obtained into the adolescent's reasoning surrounding his or her diagnosis. In this way, the clinician can learn if the teenager has a fairly genuine or sophisticated understanding of his or her problems based on actual experiences (more indicative of genuine pathology) or if the self-perceptions reflect vague, inconsistent, or coached perceptions (more likely with feigning).

Adolescents are subjected to unique pressures and influences that are distinct from those of adults. As a result, adolescent deception and malingering can also be discerned based on evidence of programming in the juvenile's responses, deference to authority or some other informant during interviewing, and signs of collusion and agreement with peers. These factors represent a second area of investigation in the clinical interview called *contextual factors*, as described in Exhibit 3.3 (see also Exhibit 2.4 for detailed presentation). Contextual factors include any outside pressures or influences and settings that are likely to have either a direct or an indirect impact on the nature of an adolescent's clinical presentation. These issues should be carefully examined to determine the degree to which a teenager's self-reports and clinical symptomatology have been shaped by these factors.

The psychosocial history is a third area to explore in the clinical interview (see Exhibit 3.3), particularly when attempting to establish the severity and course of a particular disturbance. A variety of factors can be assessed, including prior treatment records, collateral reports from parents and teachers, recent psychosocial stressors, and other data from the psychosocial history. These pieces of information can often be used to establish the consistency of a patient's statements by comparing present reports with past episodes of disturbance. Adolescent self-reports can be evaluated by comparing their content with those of collateral informants.

Each of these three factors—individual, contextual, and historical—provides useful information that complements the other. Blatant, even absurd self-reports, for example, will take on different meaning if the context is a criminal presentencing evaluation as opposed to a chaotic familial situation where one parent is severely disturbed and exhibiting psychotic symptoms. The history can provide additional guidance if in the criminal context there is no history of psychiatric treatment and in the disrupted familial context there is a history of severe abuse. In the criminal case, deliberate feigning to obtain a hospital transfer and avoid incarceration is the more likely interpretation of bizarre self-reports. In the disturbed familial context, absurd self-reports may reflect an unsophisticated, disorganized attempt to seek help in escaping a chaotic family setting by mimicking symptoms observed in a mentally ill parent. In short, the three components proposed in this framework serve to complement one another during the clinical interview.

Specific Factors in the Clinical Interview

One of the most common strategies used by individuals who are dissimulating in a clinical interview is to report symptoms or make claims that are suspect because of their bizarre nature. Some self-reports have such a minuscule or unlikely chance of being true that their credibility must be questioned. For example, Rogers and Resnick (1988) noted that improbable or absurd symptoms, overly specific symptoms, or extreme symptom severity (e.g., "These voices are killing me!") are commonly seen in individuals who attempt to malinger psychopathology. In one specific clinical case, the patient claimed that he experienced visual hallucinations on a daily basis, despite the fact that no one who was familiar with him ever saw him respond in any unusual manner. Moreover, when asked about his hallucinations, they were described in a manner that sounded familiar to the examiner because they were strikingly similar to a popular television commercial. The likelihood that the hallucinations were genuine was judged to be extremely remote.

Many blatant symptoms have been empirically shown to be associated with malingering. Cornell and Hawk (1989) found that malingerers exhibit significantly more exaggerated behaviors and bogus symptoms than do patients with genuine psychosis. Thus, the open-ended questioning of an adolescent (e.g., "What do you experience that leads you to believe you are depressed?" or "Tell me what happened" when inquiring about a particular event) is likely to elicit some of the more blatant symptoms. It is extremely important to keep questions open-ended at first to elicit spontaneous self-reports from adolescents.

Once these initial questions are asked, then more direct and specific inquiries can be made. This approach prevents contamination of the interview from such factors as the suggestibility of the teenager, efforts to "please" the examiner, and other attempts at impression management.

Subtle strategies are more difficult to detect than blatant attempts to feign mental illness. Rogers and Resnick (1988) identified two strategies that are important to use in a clinical interview: (a) comparing subtle and obvious symptoms and (b) looking for rare or unusual symptom combinations. Cornell and Hawk (1989) have found empirical support for the validity of these strategies. These researchers found a significantly higher percentage of symptoms that failed to cluster together in a sample of malingerers, but this problem never occcurred in those with genuine psychotic disturbances. In addition, Cornell and Hawk found that malingerers could mimic the content or obvious signs of mental illness, but not the more subtle forms of disturbance. Therefore, adolescents who claim to be suicidal due to severe depression, for example, and who are suspected of doing so for some secondary gain unrelated to a true major depression will be able to more readily feign obvious symptoms such as suicidal thoughts, self-reports of depressed mood, and a lack of self-reported energy. However, more subtle symptoms, such as diurnal mood variation or excessive guilt, will be less likely in cases of dissimulation. Likewise, obvious signs of psychosis (e.g., positive signs such as delusions, hallucinations) will be easier to feign than subtle symptoms (e.g., negative signs such as social withdrawl, anhedonia, autistic reasoning).

There is also a set of intermediate strategies outlined by Rogers and Resnick (1988) that is useful in the clinical interview. These strategies include (a) looking for the endorsement of rare or infrequent symptoms; (b) nonselective or indiscriminate endorsement of symptoms; (c) sudden or unusual symptom onset and resolution; (d) inconsistent or unreliable symptom reports; and (e) disparity between what the patient reports in symptoms and what the clinician actually observes. One of the main distinguishing factors of these strategies involves an erratic or inconsistent presentation of symptoms. There may be changes across time, differences between what is observed and what is reported, and other indices of unreliability in the patient's self-reports.

Another important source of information that can be useful in assessing malingering in adolescents is an exploration of their self-perceptions about the problems they are experiencing. For example, one teenager presented for an evaluation to determine the extent, if any, of injury following an accident. The likelihood of dissimulation was high, given the context, but he also had a documented history of learning disability and conduct disturbances. Following the accident in which he was struck by a car and knocked unconscious, his mother and attorney had attempted to seek a settlement, claiming that the boy suffered severe injuries from the accident. The injury was given as the cause of his learning and conduct problems, but the history revealed that these problems antedated the car accident. When interviewing this youth, the following interchange took place:

Examiner: So tell me, what's your understanding of why we are meeting?

Youth: To see if I'm hyperactive. I got a problem with hyperactivity.

Examiner: Do you know why this evaluation is being done?

Youth: To see if I should get disability.

Examiner: Tell me about this hyperactivity. What kinds of problems are you having that lead you to believe you are hyperactive?

Youth: My mother, she thinks . . . [pause] . . . I got a problem sitting still.

This interaction took place at the beginning of the examination, and the interviewee's brief reference to his mother when initially asked about his hyperactivity tipped off the examiner to the possibility that this teenager might not be experiencing clinically diagnosable hyper-activity but had been coached by his mother to provide answers that would assure him of receiving benefits. As the interview unfolded without the mother present, it became clear that the teenager did not have a perception of himself as hyperactive; indeed, he minimized several areas of concern and provided psychological test results and interview material that supported a diagnosis of conduct disorder. When explored in depth, the perception he had of himself and his problems was not that of a hyperactive child. The significance of this case illustration is that the perception an adolescent has of his or her presenting symptoms can also be very enlightening. In this case, there was evidence of symptom coaching that occurred prior to the evaluation. Explorations of the adolescent's self-perception relative to the presenting problems can offer insights into the specificity of the adolescent's experiences, genuineness of his or her affect, and other factors suggestive of feigning and dissimulation.

Contextual and Historical Factors in the Clinical Interview

With adolescents, there are several variables impacting clinical presentation, thus rendering the likelihood of some form of dissimulation more or less likely. It will be recalled from chapter 2 that peers, family members, attitudes in popular culture, and other similar issues were discussed in terms of their relevance to understanding the veracity of adolescent self-reports. In the clinical interviews, these issues are extremely important and should be explored in some detail. Therefore, an obvious area of inquiry is to explore with the adolescent his or her understanding of how peers, family, and other persons view his or her current situation. Moreover, conjoint interviews with family members and the adolescent can be instructive on various familial pressures that may have an impact on the sincerity or veracity of an adolescent's presentation.

Consider the case of John, a 16-year-old youth who was initially hospitalized for making suicide threats to his parents. The parents became sufficiently concerned to bring John to the hospital. Upon initial evaluation on the unit, he presented as an irritable, self-aggrandizing, egocentric youth from a well-to-do family who had recently gotten into a major disagreement with his parents over his wishes to transfer from one prominent private school to another. He was an only child who was idolized by his parents. There was no evidence of serious suicidal risk, as John had no prior history of attempts and he did not endorse any active suicidal intent. Essentially, the staff's initial reaction was surprise as to why John had been admitted in the first place. Only after a family meeting was held were the dynamics of his suicidal threats made clear. His parents were surprised and baffled by the threats, and they did not understand "why John could be so depressed." He interpreted his parents' reactions as insincere responses to him, and as a result of this narcissistic injury, he expressed suicidal ideation that immediately brought his parents to a state of extreme worry and anxiety. Follow-up interviews with John revealed that he was aware of these dynamics and was resistant to admit his threats were manipulative attempts to agitate his parents. In fact, he admitted to "liking himself too much" to genuinely consider taking his life.

This clinical example illustrates how family dynamics were useful in placing John's self-reports in an important context. Moreover, these dynamics served to assess the severity of his suicide threats. Although the assessment of family or peer influences may reveal symptom coaching or collusion, it also creates a background against which the adolescent's self-reports can be evaluated.

Other contextual factors can also be assessed in the clinical interview. Recall, for example, the case in chapter 2 of the teenager who became suicidal in response to her anguish over the death of an idolized rock star. Popular culture influences many teenagers to an excessive degree, and these factors, although not necessarily resulting in malingered or feigned symptoms, can distort adolescent symptoms and self-reports. These influences can be assessed by beginning with interests and hobbies the adolescent has (e.g., favorite musical groups, sports, artistic interests). Additional areas that can be assessed include friendships and group norms within one's peer group (e.g., "Who is the person you trust most?"). Assessment of these areas reveals significant information about the teenager's values regarding honesty, the likelihood of being influenced by others, conforming behavior, and other attributes that make the veracity of self-reports either more or less likely.

One feature of structured interviews that makes them well-suited for assessing the veracity of symptom self-reports is that they provide a standard method of interviewing that can be repeated across time. Consistency in self-reports is one factor that is commonly associated with truthfulness. Thus, it is an important part of any assessment to take a comprehensive psychosocial history. Advantages of a history include the ability to compare an adolescent's current functioning with periods in the past, obtaining information on prior exposure to psychopathology (i.e., through family, friends, etc.) and assessing current stressors that may maintain or contribute to current symptoms. Collateral information is extremely important, and interviews with parents, teachers, or other informants can provide corroborative or disconfirming evidence for the adolescent's self-reports. In addition, a review of documents and records can be highly useful. In forensic cases, it is extremely important to have as much collateral information and documentation as possible in order to provide the examiner with sufficient data to evaluate the veracity, accuracy, and reliability of information obtained from the clinical interview with the adolescent.

There is no set of questions that makes up a standard clinical interview for adolescents. However, rapport building, flexibility in questioning, and an appropriate mix of open-ended and close-ended questions should all be part of one's interviewing repertoire. In later discussions, I will present various in-depth case examples to illustrate some of the principles outlined in this section.

STATEMENT REALITY ANALYSIS

Assessment of the veracity, accuracy, and genuineness of statements made by adolescents is highly dependent on the context of the evaluation. In psychotherapy, for example, the interview is used to guide the patient through a discussion of various sensitive issues, with the ultimate goal being elimination of distressing symptoms. Oftentimes, the accuracy or veracity of patient self-reports is less important to the therapist than whether or not a patient believes he or she is being truthful. Once this permissive approach to truthfulness goes outside the therapist's consulting room, there is an entirely different set of assumptions and principles that apply. Failure to recognize these differences can lead to disastrous consequences, as, for example, when a therapist encourages a patient to sue a parent for civil damages based on "believed" repressed memories of childhood sexual abuse (Ofshe & Watters, 1994). When the interview is used to gather evidence for a legal proceeding, on the other hand, then veracity, accuracy, and reliability become paramount concerns. In other words, the interviewer's concern over a statement's validity and truthfulness is different in clinical and therapeutic settings than in forensically or investigatively oriented interviews.

There are a number of settings in which an adolescent is interviewed and asked to give statements concerning a specific incident or event. Among the many examples of such statements are descriptions of alleged sexual or physical abuse, confession to a crime, and a recount of witnessed events. In each of these instances, the veracity of an adolescent's statement is of primary concern.

An innovative technique for evaluating the truthfulness of a witness's statement is Statement Reality Analysis (SRA), a semiobjective method for examining verbal or written statements. Developed by the German psychologist Udo Undeutsch (1982, 1989), SRA is a technique that has specific criteria for analysis, a specific set of assumptions forming the basis for its procedures, and a growing body of research that demonstrates its promise as a useful investigative tool (Bekerian & Dennett, 1995; Gudjonsson, 1992; Horowitz, 1991).

A number of basic assumptions about human behavior and the nature of true and false statements form the basic foundation of Statement Reality Analysis (SRA). Undeutsch (1982, 1989) assumed that the best way to evaluate the truthfulness of a statement is by examining the statement itself, not the personality or reputation of the individual making the statement. The rationale behind this assumption is that individuals who are reputable and of sound moral character can, and sometimes do, make untruthful or deceptive statements, just as people of questionable character who lack credibility are capable of telling the truth. It is the content and nature of the statement that is the focus in SRA.

Another assumption underlying SRA, and one that is perhaps most important, is that truthful statements differ from untrue or deceptive statements in identifiable ways. When events are reported in a distorted or biased fashion, they are done so in a way that reveals different structure, content, and quality in the statement than do truthful accounts. Accordingly, SRA has a set of objective criteria that have been formulated as a checklist for examining and assessing the veracity of statements.

The original criteria proposed by Undeutsch serve as a set of characteristics about a statement; the more criteria that are present, the more likely a statement is truthful. Gudjonsson (1992) cited the original criteria in SRA as being (a) originality, (b) clarity, (c) vividness, (d) internal consistency, (e) detailed descriptions that are specific to the type of event that occurred, (f) reference to specific detail, (g) reporting subjective feelings, and (h) spontaneous corrections or additional information. A major criticism of these early criteria was that they lacked precision and a standard method of definition and application. Steller and Koehnken (1989) have expanded the original SRA criteria into five major dimensions of statement analysis with 19 content-based criteria that are used to analyze the statement. Exhibit 3.4 outlines the SRA criteria and provides specific definitions or examples of each.

Despite recent efforts to objectively standardize SRA criteria, there are no quantitative scoring systems or empirically based cutoffs currently available. There have been some attempts to create objective scoring criteria based on a Likert-type scale, whereby each criterion is scored on a scale from *absent* on one end to *strongly present* on the other (Raskin & Steller, 1989; Steller & Boychuck, 1992). Although these efforts hold promise, they have not achieved a satisfactory level of acceptance to warrant their adaptation in clinical settings at this time. Anson, Golding, and Gully (1993) found, for instance, that the 19 criteria outlined by Steller and Koehnken (1989) had only moderate interrater reliability when corrected for chance levels of agreement. Moreover, this study found that the criteria needed to be more explicitly defined, anchored in behavioral or verifiable criteria, and focused on identifiable problems.

SRA was originally developed as a technique for evaluating the va-

Exhibit 3.4

Statement Reality Analysis Criteria

I. General characteristics of the statement

    A. Logical structure: Examiner analyzes the way various pieces of the statement fit together; reasoning exhibited in the statement; internal consistency.

    B. Unstructured production: No preset outline unfolds; events are presented in the sequence in which they are remembered.

    C. Quantity of details: There is spontaneous production of detailed material reflecting personal connection to the event.

II. Specific contents

    D. Contextual embedding: Interviewee can describe surrounding circumstances for an event and relate them to what occurred.

    E. Description of interactions: Interviewee can describe how varous individuals related to one another (e.g., angrily, ignored one another).

    F. Reproduction of conversation: Detailed conversation can be recalled word-for-word; conversations appear original and not stilted or "canned" (e.g., "I told the teller, 'Keep your hands off the alarm and on the counter'" rather than "I said, 'This is a stick-up'").

    G. Unexpected complication during the incident: Interviewee describes something that occurred that was surprising and not expected.

III. Peculiarities of content

    H. Unusual details: Interviewee recounts observations of original, idiosyncratic details.

    I. Superfluous details: Interviewee provides extra details that create a vivid image of what occurred for the examiner.

    J. Accurately reported details misunderstood: Interviewee appears confused by some of the details recalled; no excessive attempt to explain away each and every inconsistency.

Exhibit continues

Exhibit 3.4 (*Continued*)

Statement Reality Analysis Criteria

    K. Related external associations: Interviewee connects events to those of other life experiences (e.g., "It reminded me of when …").

    L. Accounts of subjective mental state: Interviewee can relate his or her subjective impressions, feelings, etc.

    M. Attributions of perpetrator's mental state: Interviewee can describe his or her feelings about the perpetrator's feelings, impressions, etc.

IV. Motivation-related contents

    N. Spontaneous corrections: Interviewee makes subtle changes to try and assure accuracy in reporting details; this should be distinguished from a lack of internal consistency and reliability, which involves changes in major details as opposed to minor details.

    O. Admission to lack of memory: Interviewee does not attempt to account for each and every detail; admits those details that he or she is not sure about and attempts to maintain a level of accuracy.

    P. Self-doubts about one's testimony: Interviewee admits or concedes legitimate doubts when they exist.

    Q. Self-deprecation: Interviewee does not attempt to "know it all"; is apologetic for details that cannot be recalled.

    R. Forgiving/pardoning of perpetrator: Interviewee minimizes or makes excuses for wrongful behavior of others who have committed a wrong.

V. Offense-specific elements

    S. Details are characteristic of offense: Details are not absurd and do not defy logic about the event (e.g., reports of being anally penetrated with a knife blade in the absence of any medical evidence of injury).

lidity of children's claims of sexual abuse. However, the technique has potential application in any setting in which a juvenile's description of an event or set of facts is the focus. Preliminary validity data suggest promising results. For example, raters trained in SRA were able to accurately differentiate all statements made by children in confirmed cases of sexual abuse from those made by children in unconfirmed statements (Raskin & Esplin, 1991). However, these results have not been cross-validated, and some of the 19 SRA criteria worked well, whereas others did not. More distressing is the fact that SRA was not able to successfully distinguish genuine from fabricated reports of child sexual abuse when subjects were "coached" to provide specific details and information (findings reported in Bekerian & Dennett, 1995). Better results are obtained, however, when studies examine the 19 individual SRA content criteria, something that those studies with disappointing findings did not do. Bekerian and Dennett described research findings that showed that nine SRA criteria effectively distinguished genuine and fabricated statements from one another in that the nine criteria were absent from fabricated statements. These nine criteria were logical consistency, perceptual details, embedding, complications, unusual details, superfluous details, misunderstood details, association, and self-deprecation. The criteria that did not help to distinguish true from false statements were the motivation-related criteria listed in Exhibit 3.4 (Bekerian & Dennett, 1995).

Porter and Yuille (1996) found that SRA (or Statement Validity Analysis [SVA], as these authors refer to the procedure) performed better than three other methods for detecting deception in the identification of false confessions. The three other methods examined included reality monitoring (Johnson & Raye, 1981), scientific content analysis, and lexical diversity. Each of these approaches examines the structure of language used in a particular statement, such as the number of connectors used (e.g., *next, after*), pauses, and references to self (e.g., *I, me*). The best clues to deception were three criteria from SRA, which included the Quality of Details, Logical Structure (i.e., coherence), and Admission of Lack of Memory.

An important finding in SRA validity research is that younger children generally have fewer SRA criteria in their truthful statements than do older children (Bekerian & Dennett, 1995). That is, age is positively correlated with the number and strength of ratings for the criteria. Conceptually and theoretically, this trend makes sense, since as children develop into adolescence, their cognitive abilities expand to account for better recall of detail, greater complexity in reasoning and verbal skills, and more spontaneity in the recollection of events. Because SRA is greatly influenced by age, many of the serious questions arise over its accuracy and utility with younger children. The cognitive capacities of adolescents are similar to those of adults; thus, SRA is a potentially valuable tool for analyzing statement validity in teenagers.

As noted earlier, the major drawback to SRA is the fact that there is no standard scoring method available for analyzing each of the content criteria and no empirically based cutoffs have been developed or cross-validated. Therefore, as a technique in clinical or forensic evaluation, SRA cannot stand alone; proper application of the criteria requires experience with their use. Another potential limitation of SRA is that although it may be able to assist in distinguishing true from fabricated statements, it remains untested for identifying true and fabricated components in statements that have elements of both truth and dishonesty. Based on available research, SRA criteria may serve as a useful guideline for analyzing adolescent statements such as sworn confessions, allegations of abuse, and other accounts of significant events. Use of the criteria as a guideline can provide corroborative evidence for other data such as testing results, psychosocial history, record and document review, and collateral interviews. Even as a general guideline, however, SRA criteria demand that certain procedures and principles be followed to assure their prudent use with adolescents. At a minimum, the following criteria should be satisfied:

1. The interviewer should be experienced and have basic skill in interviewing adolescents.
2. Rapport should be obtained prior to obtaining the statement to be analyzed (e.g., hobbies, interests, or other innocuous topics).
3. The adolescent should be asked general, nonleading questions about the incident to get a sample of his or her narrative style.

4. Specific questions should be used sparingly at first; only later should questions be used (e.g., "What was said?" or "What were you feeling?") to illumine specific SRA criteria in material elicited in the initial reports.
5. Every effort should be made to have a preserved copy of the statement through audio- or videotaping, transcription, the interviewee's own handwriting, or detailed note taking with direct quotes.
6. The interviewer should have factual knowledge of the alleged event (i.e., collateral reports, police reports, etc.).
7. The interviewer should have knowledge of the research pertaining to the event under investigation (e.g., realistic symptoms associated with a particular diagnosis, suggestibility and coercion in confessions, memory).
8. Detailed knowledge of the circumstances under which a statement was obtained for those cases where the clinician was not directly involved in obtaining the statement.

Athough other relevant factors of the interview are important, such as those individual, contextual, and historical issues discussed earlier, application of SRA requires a certain degree of structure to the interview. As with all interviewing procedures, the examiner is wise to have a general framework and to monitor his or her influences on the dynamics of the interview. SRA is not a panacea and it cannot stand alone as a technique for making definitive statements regarding the veracity of adolescent self-reports. Used cautiously, conservatively, and prudently, however, it can serve as a useful adjunct to clinical interviewing.

CONCLUSION

The interview has long been considered the primary method for gathering information about an individual's level of functioning and presenting symptomatology. With respect to evaluating malingering and deception, the traditional clinical interview is an integral part of the assessment, but by itself, it is inadequate for identifying malingering and deception. In recent years, the development of structured clinical interviews has provided practitioners with useful ancillary techniques to support the traditional interview, and they have potential for increasing the reliability and validity of clinical diagnosis.

Two structured interviews, the SIRS and PCL–R, have particular relevance to evaluating malingering and deception. Although there is a severe lack of published research on adolescent populations, recent findings suggest that the SIRS is valid in teenage populations and can be used to corroborate findings and hypotheses generated from a complete psychological evaluation. The PCL–R may be useful for evaluating lying and deception associated with severe personality disorders associated with psychopathy.

A framework is also provided to help clinicians structure their clinical interviews based on factors associated with the adolescent's manner of presentation, overt self-report style, and perception of his or her current circumstances. Another technique that has shown promise is SRA. This is a highly specialized technique for analyzing verbal statements obtained from unstructured or open-ended interviews.

Again, the interview is extremely important in the assessment of malingering and deception, but alone, it has not proven extremely effective in providing all the information necessary to make an accurate determination of malingering or deception. Some of the more important information that can be obtained through traditional clinical interviewing is the contextual and historical factors, whereas structured interviews provide information on self-report styles. Another key piece of information is psychological testing results, the focus of the next chapter.

4

Psychological Testing Approaches

The use of standardized psychological tests is considered by many to be one of the more effective methods for identifying malingering and deception in clinical assessment. One of the main reasons for wide interest in the use of psychological tests is that much of the empirical research on dissimulation has focused on the use of such tests as the MMPI in identifying various response styles. Psychological test results permit more objective analysis of an individual's responses, and they reflect an organized sample of behavior that can be readily represented in the form of quantifiable scores on a standardized scale. For these reasons, psychological tests represent the most extensively researched techniques for identifying and classifying malingerers.

The amount of empirical research available on any psychometric test is a major factor that must be taken into account when evaluating its utility for clinical assessment purposes. In the last chapter, I pointed out that several structured interview methods are available for assisting with the evaluation of dissimulation. However, with the exception of the SIRS, which is a structured interview method, there has been no experimental evidence supporting the unstructured clinical interview as a method for differentiating bona fide from malingered mental disorders (Ziskin, 1984). There are, however, controlled studies examining the use of psychological tests in differentiating malingered and genuine psychological disturbances. A variety of experimental designs have been used in research (Schretlen, 1988). In many studies, for example, the psychological test results of "suspected" malingerers are compared with results from patients with "genuine" disturbances. Other experimental designs involve simulation procedures whereby experimental participants (either normal or patient populations) are instructed to take a psychological test under honest conditions and again under a specific instructional set (i.e., either "fake good" or "fake bad"). The inclusion of several respondent groups, such as suspected malingerers, bona fide patients, normal controls, and respondents who simulate illness according to specific instructions, helps to illuminate the degree to which test results are the product of malingering or genuine psychopathology.

According to a review of the empirical literature on detecting malingering with psychological tests, Schretlen (1988) has concluded that there is support for the validity of tests in differentiating genuine and malingered mental disorders. In fact, he concluded that "it is probably indefensible to render expert testimony regarding the likelihood of malingering unless one has psychological test data that bear on the question" (p. 473). Therefore, the use of psychological testing is a core component of any evaluation that has dissimulation or malingering as a major issue.

There are a number of issues that arise when psychological tests are used to answer clinical questions, and many of these issues are more pronounced when tests are applied in the area of forensic assessment. In short, strict reliance on specific psychological test scores for drawing conclusions about a particular individual is improper and prone to error unless such scores are interpreted in the context of what is known about the individual's prior life experiences, current life circumstances, and other data from the assessment (Matarazzo, 1990). It could be stated that psychological test scores are meaningless, in themselves, without the individual's history, assessment context, and other relevant information. Thus, psychological tests are not useful when used in a mechanized fashion that is isolated from the patient's history and contextual setting; this integrative approach to assessment is one reason that contextual factors were emphasized earlier during the discussion of theoretical models of malingering.

Another major issue in psychological testing involves the proper standardization of a test and subsequent application to an individual that is represented in the sample against which the test was validated. This issue is extremely important, particularly when evaluating adolescents. The history of psychological testing reveals that adolescents were once thought to be mini-adults who experienced many of the same clinical problems as did adults. As a result, many tests that were validated on adults (e.g., MMPI) were merely administered to adolescents with perhaps some minor changes in normative conversion data or scoring algorithms (Archer & Ball, 1988; McCann, 1997). However, this approach to psychological testing of adolescents was fraught with numerous limitations. As we have seen in chapter 1, adolescence is a phase of human development that has a unique series of physiological, psychological, and social processes that make it worthy of special consideration. Therefore, psychological tests designed for or normed on adolescent populations are preferred. In forensic settings, where malingering and deception are frequent and significant considerations, the applicability of a test to the population being evaluated (i.e., adolescents) is a major factor in guiding test selection (Heilbrun, 1992). Therefore, any psychological test that is used to assess malingering or dissimulation in adolescents should be designed for use with that age group, have well-established adolescent norms, and have validation research supporting its ability to differentiate among various response sets, including malingering and dissimulation.

One major difficulty in the area of psychological testing of adolescents is that only within the last decade or so has there been any effort to develop tests specifically for this age group. What complicates the issue further is the fact that, as mentioned in chapter 2, most research on malingering and deception has focused exclusively on adults. In recent years, there have been some gains made toward looking more closely at adolescent malingering, but the research remains scant.

In this chapter, various psychological tests will be reviewed as they bear on the assessment of adolescent malingering and dissimulation. Two broad categories of tests are personality measures and cognitive, neuropsychological, or intellectual measures. Most of the research has focused on the former, including the MMPI–A, MACI, and Rorschach (Exner & Weiner, 1982). Each of these instruments will therefore be reviewed with respect to its utility in assessing adolescent dissimulation. A section on cognitive, intellectual, and neuropsychological assessment will also be presented.

THE MINNESOTA MULTIPHASIC PERSONALITY INVENTORY–ADOLESCENT (MMPI–A)

The MMPI–A is a 478-item personality inventory that is designed for teenagers 14 to 18 years old. Separate norms exist for boys and girls, and, based on an analysis of reading difficulty, the recommended standard for proper administration of the test calls for a seventh-grade reading level (Archer, 1992; Butcher et al., 1992). The MMPI–A is a recently developed revision of the MMPI, which for years was the standard objective personality instrument in psychology. Concerns over the inappropriateness of measuring adolescent personality with an instrument designed primarily for adults, the lack of scales on the original MMPI for assessing specific adolescent problems, and the lack of an adequate adolescent normative sample all spurred efforts to produce the MMPI–A.

Among those clinicians who evaluate adolescents, the MMPI ranked sixth among all tests and first among all objective personality measures that were cited as the most frequently used tests in adolescent assessment (Archer, Maruish, Imhof, & Piotrowski, 1991). Thus, there is substantial interest in use of the MMPI–A in clinical practice. In terms of malingering and dissimulation assessment, the MMPI–A is of even greater importance due to the existence of several response style and validity scales that are designed to measure such tendencies as inconsistent responding, over- or underreporting of pathology, and various other response sets. The assessment of response style has direct relevance to the issue of malingering, defensiveness, and distorted self-

Table 4.1

MMPI–A Measures for Assessing Self-Report Style and Profile Validity

Scale/ Measure	Description	Definition
?	Cannot Say	Total number of items either left blank or answered both True and False.
L	Lie	Measures naive or unsophisticated attempts to put forth an unrealistically positive presentation.
F	Infrequency	Measures attempts to put forth an unfavorable presentation, overreporting of pathology, "faking bad."
F_1	Infrequency (Front)	Scale F items from the first half of the test (Items 1–350).
F_2	Infrequency (Back)	Scale F items from the last half of the test (Items 242–478).
K	Defensiveness	Measures defensiveness, social desirability, and tendencies to "fake good."
VRIN	Variable Response Inconsistency	Measures tendencies to respond inconsistently.
TRIN	True Response Inconsistency	Indiscriminate responding due to answering either all True or all False.

reports (Heilbrun, 1992; Marlowe, 1995). Table 4.1 outlines the major MMPI–A validity indices and scales that are used in evaluating the reliability and accuracy of adolescent self-reports. Although these scales are standard indices, other measures of profile validity, initially developed on adult populations, have been studied in adolescent populations.

Archer (1987) reported on the use of the MMPI validity scale with adolescents and found that measures of defensiveness (scales L and K) were essentially equivalent in adolescent and adult populations. However, scale *F* demonstrated significantly higher elevations in adolescent populations when compared with those of adults. In fact, different cut-off scores were recommended for adults and adolescents on scale *F* when making decisions about MMPI profile validity (Archer, 1984; Marks, Seeman, & Haller, 1974). In short, adolescents reported more infrequent or unusual symptomatology on the MMPI than did adults. The degree to which this phenomenon is due to reading difficulties, age differences, or other developmental processes as opposed to greater psychopathology in teenagers remains a matter of professional debate.

Other attempts have been carried out to investigate the ability of the MMPI validity scales to detect invalid self-report styles in adolescents. Archer, Gordon, and Kirchner (1987) found that "all-true" and "all-false" profiles are the same in adolescents and adults, whereas adolescents provide a random response set that is unique to that age group. Additionally, Archer and his colleagues found that the MMPI validity scales *(L, F,* and *K)* are useful in detecting fake-bad profiles, whereas fake-good profiles are more difficult to detect. Attempts to expand the range of possible validity indices on the original MMPI with adolescents have yielded disappointing results. Although the use of subtle items (i.e., items having little face validity but adequate criterion validity) has been useful in detecting deception in adults (Dannenbaum & Lanyon, 1993), the use of such items does not appear to provide any additional diagnostic power with adolescent populations (Herkov, Archer, & Gordon, 1991).

Based on the limited research findings on MMPI validity scales and adolescent response sets, the MMPI–A relies heavily on the traditional validity scales *(L, F,* and *K)*, along with some newer scales, including F_1 *(F-front)* and F_2 *(F-back), VRIN,* and *TRIN.* These scales are all defined in Table 4.1. According to Archer (1992), the committee that restandardized the MMPI to produce the MMPI–A did not include such validity scales as the Wiener-Harmon Subtle–Obvious subscales (Wiener, 1948) because of the lack of empirical support for these measures in detecting deception in adolescent populations. Likewise, there has been insufficient research to support the use of such indices as critical items (Archer & Jacobson, 1993). Although Archer (1992) also cautioned against the use of the F-minus-K index for evaluating MMPI−A validity, Rogers et al. (1996) found this validity index to have the most promise of all MMPI−A validity indicators in detecting adolescent malingering. Additional support for using the F-minus-K index to classify fake-bad MMPI−A profiles in adolescents has also been obtained by Stein, Graham, and Williams (1995). However, most interpretive guides to using the MMPI−A for detecting deception have recommended use of the basic validity scales listed in Table 4.1 (Archer, 1992; Butcher et al., 1992; Pope, Butcher, & Seelen, 1993). Attempts to develop additional measures of MMPI−A profile validity, such as Items-Easy and Items-Difficult subscales to evaluate the impact of reading comprehension difficulties on scale F elevations, have met with inconsistent results (Krakauer, Archer, & Gordon, 1993). The most promising results to date on the assessment of adolescent malingering have been obtained by Rogers et al. (1996) using the F-minus-K index on the MMPI−A and by Stein et al. (1995) using both the F-minus-K index and scale F raw score.

At the present time, research on MMPI−A validity scales and the detection of malingering, denial, and dissimulation supports use of the scales listed in Table 4.1 as confirmatory data and not as definitive measures of these self-report styles in adolescents. Promising results have been found for the F-minus-K index and scale F, suggesting that these pieces of data may add to the assessment of malingering in particular.

Cannot Say *(?)* Score

In a technical sense, the Cannot Say *(?)* score on the MMPI−A is not a scale but is rather the number of items left blank or double-marked as both True and False. Archer (1992) cited the following interpretive guidelines for the Cannot Say *(?)* score. Raw scores of 0 to 3 are considered "Low" and reflect a willingness to respond to items and a lack of evasiveness. Scores in the 4 to 10 range are considered "Moderate" and may reflect selective responding or limited experiences to draw upon when answering questions. When raw scores fall in the 11 to 30 range, there is "Marked" resistance or indecision in responding that have an adverse effect on profile configuration. Archer considers Cannot Say *(?)* raw scores of 31 and above as reflecting "Invalid" MMPI–A profiles due to defiance, reading difficulties, lack of cooperation, or resistance to self-disclosure. Accordingly, the Cannot Say *(?)* score is correlated with intellectual functioning and reading ability; therefore, elevations on this measure should be interpreted carefully within the context of available data on the teenager's educational background and intellectual–cognitive capabilities.

Lie *(L)* Scale

Contrary to what is implied by the name of this scale, the *L* scale is not a measure of lying tendencies and is not a crude "lie detector." Thus, one should carefully correct any attorney, lay observer, or other individual who attempts to construe the scale as a lie detector. The *L* scale is designed as a measure of denial, lack of insight, or unsophisticated attempts to put oneself in a positive light. When T-score values are equal to or below 45, the score reflects openness in self-reporting, whereas T-scores above 65 reflect denial, a lack of insight, and superficial attempts to present a positive picture of oneself (Archer, 1992; Butcher et al., 1992). T-scores in the 46-to-55 range are considered "Normal" and those in the 56-to-65 range are Moderate and reflect a tendency toward conforming and conventional behavior (Archer, 1992).

Infrequency *(F)* Scale

This scale was originally designed by selecting those items on the MMPI that were endorsed infrequently, or less than 10% of the time by the normative sample. On the MMPI–A, items were selected for inclusion if they had an endorsement frequency of less than 20% by the normative sample. In adolescent populations, this scale is problematic because respondents in this age group produce rather high elevations on scale *F* (Archer, 1987, 1992), so it is curious that an endorsement frequency of 20% was chosen for inclusion of an item on scale *F* on the MMPI–A. Because this scale is designed to measure unusual symptoms or the overreporting of bizarre problems, a more rational criterion would have been a *lower* cutoff (e.g., 5% endorsement frequency). That

Table 4.2

Accuracy of MMPI–A Scales and Indices for Detecting Malingering

Cutoff	PPP	NPP
F-minus-K[a]		
>10	0.91	0.59
>20	0.83	0.91
Scale F T-Score[a]		
>81	0.66	0.91
Scale F Raw Score[b]		
≥23	0.94	0.89

NOTE: PPP = positive predictive power; NPP = negative predictive power. (See chap. 5 in this book for a complete description of these terms).
[a]Base rate of malingering = 50%; data are from Rogers, Hinds, and Sewell (1996).
[b]Base rate of malingering = 33%; data are from Stein, Graham, and Williams (1995).

is, because adolescents tend to report more unusual symptoms on the MMPI than do adults, scale F should be designed specifically for adolescents in order for it to be a measure of extreme or bizarre responding. Nevertheless, the scale is designed to be a measure of overreporting of psychopathology. According to Archer (1992), T-score elevations in the 66 to 89 range are taken to reflect Marked elevations that are indicative of significant psychopathology. A T-score on scale F of 90 and above is considered "Extreme" and is recommended as a cutoff for profile invalidity that is due to severe disorganization, malingering, or psychosis. However, Rogers et al. (1996) found that because of poor positive predictive power, the T-score of 90 cutoff on MMPI–A scale F was ineffective in identifying adolescent malingerers.

Less extreme cutoffs on scale F appear to have greater efficacy in identifying malingered or fake-bad profiles. For instance, Rogers et al. (1996) found respectable results with scale F when a T-score cutoff of greater than 81 was used. Table 4.2 provides the positive and negative predictive power of this cutoff to be 0.66 and 0.91 respectively. Although I will discuss these interpretive statistics more fully in chapter

5, a brief interpretation of these statistics is that with a population base rate of 50%,[1] there is a 66% chance that an adolescent scoring above a T-score of 81 on scale F is malingering and a 91% chance that an adolescent scoring below this cutoff is not malingering. Both of these cutoffs operate at better than chance levels, since one would expect a 50% chance of correct classification based on a random assignment of adolescents to either honest or dissimulating conditions. As Rogers and his colleagues cautioned, however, these results are prone to "overfitting" the data because the cutoff is the one that provided maximum discrimination in the experimental situation.

Better results on the accuracy of scale F in identifying fake-bad profiles have been obtained by Stein et al. (1995). By expanding on results obtained by Archer and colleagues (1987), Stein and colleagues examined the effectiveness of the raw score of scale F as a measure of fake-bad responding. With the base rate of malingering experimentally set at 33%, Stein and colleagues found that a raw score of $F \geq 23$ yielded a positive predictive power of 0.94 and a negative predictive power of 0.89. Although the base rate of negative response styles was extremely high, this cutoff appears very promising and can provide confirmatory data of malingering that well exceeds chance levels. Table 4.2 summarizes the various cutoffs that have been derived for scale F on the MMPI–A.

Defensiveness (K) Scale

The items comprising scale K on the MMPI–A are essentially the same as those on the original MMPI. Selection of items on this scale were originally based on their ability to identify individuals with prominent levels of psychopathology who had profiles in the normal range. Scale K is designed to measure social desirability, psychological defensiveness, and other tendencies toward avoiding self-disclosure. Accordingly, Archer (1992) has recommended a cutoff of T = 66 and above to denote

---

[1] Rogers et al. (1996) used a within-subjects design whereby participants took the MMPI–A under both honest and dissimulating conditions. Therefore, the "malingering" base rate, or number of participants in the sample who were actually dissimulating in the negative direction, was 50%.

Marked levels of defensiveness. Scores in this range are linked to poor prognosis in psychotherapy and with a fake-good response set.

VRIN and TRIN

Of no small concern in the assessment of self-report validity are the influences of inconsistent and unreliable responding. The Variable Response Inconsistency *(VRIN)* and True Response Inconsistency *(TRIN)* scales of the MMPI–A are two recent additions to the MMPI literature and are designed to evaluate conflicting or antithetical self-reports. Composed of 50 pairs of items with similar or divergent content, *VRIN* measures the adolescent's tendency to endorse statements, symptoms, or personality features that are inconsistent with one another. For example, an adolescent who responds True to the statement, "I am always happy" and False to "Most of the time I am content" would be providing inconsistent self-reports. The raw score for *VRIN* is the number of pairs of statements reflecting divergent responding; this score is then converted to a T-score. Given the fact that these scales are new, no research is available beyond that in the manual on appropriate cutoffs for identifying random or inconsistent responding. Different interpretive levels have been developed. For instance, Butcher and Williams (1992) recommended T-scores on *VRIN* in the 70-to-74 range as "suggestive" of invalidity due to inconsistent self-reports and T-scores of 75 or greater as indicative of invalidity. Archer (1992), on the other hand, recommended that scores in the 70-to-79 range represent "marginal" levels of inconsistency and scores of 80 or greater represent invalid profiles. For current applications, adoption of the more conservative T = 80 cutoff recommended by Archer is likely to maximize the true positive rate while lowering the true negative rate. Adoption of Butcher and Williams' T = 75 cutoff is likely to raise sensitivity at the expense of scale specificity (See chap. 5 for an explanation of these terms and principles). Further research is needed to clarify which cutoff level is most appropriate.

The *TRIN* scale is similar to *VRIN*, with the major difference being that the 20-item pairs that compose this measure are keyed so that the same response (i.e., True–True or False–False) reflects inconsistent responding. As a result, *TRIN* is useful in identifying those inconsistent response styles that are due to a mostly True (acquiescing) or mostly False (naysaying) response tendency. Again, the lack of independent research on this scale has led to different suggested cutoffs. Archer (1992) recommended the same levels for *TRIN* as he did for *VRIN* (T = 70–79 represents marginal inconsistency; T ≥ 80 reflects invalidity), as did Butcher and Williams (1992; T = 70–74 represents suspected inconsistency; T ≥ 75 reflects invalidity).

F-Minus-*K* Index

In the MMPI literature, a dissimulation index known as *F*-minus-*K* has received considerable attention as a measure of response styles, including denial and malingering (Gough, 1950; Graham, 1987, 1990; Greene, 1988, 1991). This dissimulation index is calculated by subtracting the *raw score* of *K* from that of *F*. Although Archer (1987, 1992) found this index to have little utility with adolescents and thus advised against its use, some recent data by Rogers et al. (1996) reveal that *F*-minus-*K* is perhaps the best MMPI–A measure for identifying malingering. Table 4.2 presents data from the study by Rogers and his colleagues. Examination of the table reveals that an *F*-minus-*K* cutoff greater than 20 yielded very respectable positive predictive power (0.83), which represents the likelihood that an adolescent will be correctly classified as malingering if the *F*-minus-*K* index is greater than 20. This cutoff also has respectable negative predictive power (0.91), which is the likelihood that an adolescent with *F*-minus-*K* less than 20 will be correctly classified as not malingering. Because the cutoff of 20 is the optimal criterion in this study, these predictive powers may be overestimates of actual classificatory rates; thus this cutoff requires cross-validation. Until such data are available, the *F*-minus-*K* index may again be useful in the corroboration of malingering in adolescents.

THE MILLON ADOLESCENT CLINICAL INVENTORY (MACI)

The MACI is a 160-item personality inventory that shares some features of the MMPI–A. In particular, the MACI is an objective inventory that is designed to assess clinical symptomatology and personality character-istics in adolescents. However, there are significant differences between the MACI and MMPI–A that render them very distinct psychological test instruments. Because the measurement of clinical problems and psychopathology is a major focus of the MACI, the normative sample from which the instrument was developed was drawn from adolescent inpatient, outpatient, correctional, and residential treatment programs. Thus, the MACI and MMPI–A have very different normative samples. Another major difference between the MACI and the MMPI–A is that profiles for each instrument are plotted along very different raw score conversion scales. Whereas the MMPI–A assumes a normal distribution of underlying constructs being measured, the MACI base rate (BR) score conversions are based on prevalence rates of various syndromes, clinical concerns, and personality traits among clinical populations.

There are 31 scales on the MACI that are organized into four major categories: Modifier Indices, Personality Patterns, Expressed Concerns, and Clinical Syndromes (McCann, 1997; Millon, 1993). In terms of assessing malingering and dissimulation, the Modifier Indices are four of the MACI scales that are of most relevance. The four scales mea-suring self-report style are scales VV (Reliability), X (Disclosure), Y (Desirability), and Z (Debasement). Interpretation of scales X, Y, and Z is based on BR scores, which are scores based on prevalence rates of particular disorders and conditions in the normative sample. Base rate scores differ from T-scores in that they do not assume a normal dis-tribution of the construct being measured (See McCann & Dyer, 1996 for a more complete discussion of BR scores). Table 4.3 provides a brief description for each of the Modifier Indices on the MACI, and Table 4.4 provides percentages of the normative sample falling within a given range on each scale. It should be noted that the BR cutoff scores for the MACI Modifier Indices are defined according to percentiles, with scores below a BR of 35 representing the lower 15% of the normative sample, scores between a BR of 35 and 74 representing the middle 50% of the sample, scores above a BR of 75 representing the top 25% of the normative sample, and scores above a BR of 85 representing the top 10% of the normative sample.

	Table 4.3	

MACI Measures for Assessing Self-Report Style and Profile Validity

Scale/Measure	Description	Definition
VV	Reliability	Measures unreliable self-reports due to confusion, reading/concentration problems, oppositionality, random responding, etc.
X	Disclosure	Measures overall level of openness, from nondisclosing/secretive/guarded on one end to very disclosing/complaining/exaggerating on the other end.
Y	Desirability	Measures social desirability, denial, "faking good," etc.
Z	Debasement	Measures overreporting, exaggeration, malingering, "cry for help," etc.

At the present time, there is very little empirical research on the MACI Modifier Indices, so interpretation of these scales must be carried out by examining data available in the manual, as well as by rational analysis of specific scale configurations. What follows is a brief description of each scale and a strategy for making effective use of each in the assessment of response styles.

Omitted Items

The MACI manual (Millon, 1993) notes that computerized reports provided by the test publisher, NCS Assessments, are terminated if the adolescent leaves 10 or more items blank or double-marked on the MACI answer sheet. However, McCann and Dyer (1996) have noted that with 160 items used to score 31 scales, the MACI makes maximum use of each and every item. As a general guideline, therefore, it is recommended that all items be answered by the adolescent in clinical and forensic evaluations. If an adolescent leaves any items blank or double-

Table 4.4

Frequency Table of BR Scores for MACI Scales X, Y, and Z

BR Score range	Scale		
	X	Y	Z
0–35	13.0%	12.1%	6.4%
35–74	62.7%	66.1%	72.5%
75–84	14.0%	13.1%	11.9%
85–115	10.4%	8.6%	9.2%

NOTE: From the *Millon Adolescent Clinical Inventory Manual* (p. 30), by T. Millon, 1993, Minneapolis, MN: National Computer Systems. Copyright 1993 by Theodore Millon. Used by permission of National Computer Systems, Minneapolis, MN.

marked, he or she should be asked to go back and provide a response to make sure that all items are answered appropriately.

Reliability (VV) Scale

The Reliability Index consists of two items (114 and 126) on the MACI that have extremely bizarre content. Selection of these two items was based on their very low endorsement frequencies, even among very disturbed adolescents. The MACI manual and interpretive report utilize cutoffs on this index such that if both items are endorsed, the resulting profile is considered invalid; if one of the scale VV items is endorsed, it represents a profile of questionable validity (Millon, 1993). Endorsement of either of these items is strongly suggestive of unreliable or inconsistent responding, including random responding, extreme oppositionality, reading or concentration problems, or mental confusion. Independent research by Bagby, Gillis, and Rogers (1991) has shown that this same index on the adult Millon instrument, the Millon Clinical Multiaxial Inventory–II (MCMI–II; Millon, 1987), accurately identifies more than 95% of all random response sets when a cutoff of *one item* is used. The two items making up scale VV on the MACI are also used on the MCMI–II version, thus supporting application of the findings from the study by Bagby and his colleagues to the MACI. Therefore, if only one scale *VV* item is endorsed in the True direction, the MACI profile should be considered invalid due to random responding, reading or concentration difficulties, confusion, or some other process adversely impacting the consistency and reliability of the adolescent's self-reports.

An alternative approach to interpreting scale *VV* on the MACI is to use it in screening for potential malingering. Recall from chapter 2 that Rogers' proposed model of malingering pointed out the endorsement of absurd or preposterous symptoms as a pattern of self-reporting that is commonly seen in malingerers (see Table 2.3). Endorsement of an item suggesting that the adolescent has not seen an automobile in 10 years (Item 114) or has taken an airplane flight across the Atlantic over 30 times in a year (Item 126) may be suggestive, but not conclusive, of malingering, given the bizarre and preposterous content of the items. Therefore, scale *VV* has two potential meanings if one or more items are endorsed: inconsistent or unreliable self-reports or possible malingering.

Disclosure *(X)* Scale

This scale is not a traditional psychometric scale in the sense that it is composed of specific items tapping a psychological construct. Rather, scale *X* is calculated by taking the differentially weighted raw scores of the MACI Personality Patterns scales and totaling them to obtain the raw score for scale *X*. Generally, this scale is intended to measure a teenager's openness and willingness to disclose personal concerns. According to Millon (1993), there is a high positive correlation with scale *Z* (Debasement; 0.78) and a moderate negative correlation with scale *Y* (Desirability; −0.44). Low scores on scale *X* reflect a teenager who is defensive, nondisclosing, and unwilling to reveal much about himself or herself. Among the reasons encountered for this lack of openness is a concern over how information will be used, a motivation to appear well-adjusted, or the general lack of trust adolescents often have for adults. Elevations on scale *X* reflect openness, the need to seek attention or support, directness in self-reports, or motivation to achieve some secondary gain.

Millon (1993) recommended two cutoff levels for scale X based on the inability of the MACI to maintain levels of diagnostic accuracy outside a given range of scores on the scale. Moreover, scale X is the only other Modifier Index besides scale VV that will invalidate the MACI profile according to the computerized scoring algorithms. When the *raw score* of scale X falls below 201, the MACI is considered invalid due to denial, underreporting of problems, faking good, or a similar response style that reflects an unwillingness to be open and forthright. When the *raw score* of scale X is greater than 589, the MACI is considered to be invalid due to overreporting of symptoms, a "cry for help," malingering, or some other response style based on the need to be overly disclosing of clinical symptoms.

Desirability *(Y)* Scale

This scale is comprised of 17 items that were drawn from other scales on the MACI, particularly scales 4 (Dramatizing), 5 (Egotistic), and 7 (Conforming). High scores on scale Y will also tend to be associated with an elevation on one or more of these personality scales. Based on the fact that this scale was constructed using items from scales measuring personality styles, there is a trait-oriented social desirability construct that is often, but not always associated with scale Y elevations. When compared to the empirically derived L and K scales of the MMPI–A, the trait-oriented aspects of MACI scale Y can be used to help explain atypical results in cases where an adolescent may elevate a social desirability scale on one instrument and not the other.

Elevations of BR $\geq$ 75 on scale Y reflect a need on the part of the adolescent to be viewed as well-adjusted, likeable, or without personal faults. As elevations increase, there is a more unrealistic self-appraisal and personal concerns are denied or minimized. By itself, a scale Y elevation will not invalidate the computerized interpretation of the MACI (Millon, 1993). However, McCann (1997; McCann & Dyer, 1996) has suggested that when the BR score of scale Y reaches 90, a socially desirable response set should be considered as evidence suggesting profile invalidity because the adolescent has answered almost all questions on scale Y in the affirmative and elevations on scale Y that are above a BR of 90 constitute scores above the 95th percentile. The exception to this rule would be a MACI profile that is inconsistent with social desirability (e.g. elevations on scales measuring anxiety, depression, self-deprecation) or profiles that are consistent with data from the psychosocial history and clinical presentation.

Debasement *(Z)* Scale

The Debasement scale is made up of 16 items that were drawn from other scales on the MACI, particularly scales *2B* (Doleful), *8B* (Self-Demeaning), and *B* (Self-Devaluation). Scale *Z* is designed to measure response styles that are guided by motivations to present problems and concerns in a very negative light. High scores are suggestive of over-reporting of problems, symptom exaggeration, a "cry for help," extreme distress, or malingering. Because many of the items from this scale were drawn from measures of personality styles, scale *Z* may at times show elevations that are not corroborated by other response style measures such as MMPI–A scale *F*. In these unusual situations, the differences can be explained on the basis of trait-oriented constructs being tapped by scale *Z*.

Similar to scale *Y*, scale *Z* is not used to invalidate the MACI computerized interpretive report or profile (Millon, 1993). However, it has been suggested that BR scores of 90 or above can be used to invalidate the MACI based on overreporting of symptoms, malingering, exaggeration, or a similar response set (McCann, 1997; McCann & Dyer, 1996). Elevations above a BR of 90 on scale *Z* also represent scores that fall above the 95th percentile. Exceptions to this rule would be MACI profiles that are inconsistent with overreporting (e.g., elevations on dramatizing and egotistic personality scales) or profiles that are consistent with the adolescent's psychosocial history and clinical presentation.

Modifying Indices Configurations

A valid MACI profile can be quickly identified by observing scales *X*, *Y*, and *Z* all falling below a BR score of 75 while the raw score of scale *X* remains above 200. Defensive response styles that reflect denial or other forms of dissimulation aimed at concealing personal problems will be identified by scale Y being elevated above a BR of 75 and scales X and Z falling below 75. Response styles that may be indicative of malingering, overreporting, or symptom exaggeration are identified by an elevation on scale Z above a BR of 75, with scale X typically showing an elevation as well; scale Y would fall below 75. In some cases, both scales Y (Desirability) and Z (Debasement) will be elevated at a level exceeding a BR of 75. This configuration is very unusual and reflects conflicting and inconsistent self-reports, similar to *VRIN* and *TRIN* elevations on the MMPI–A. Under these conditions, the adolescent is endorsing symptoms that are antithetical to one another (e.g., "I feel great most of the time" and "I have always been a sad person."). When *both* scales Y and Z equal or exceed a BR of 75, this measure can be used along with scale *VV* as an indication of possible inconsistent or unreliable self-reporting on the MACI.

A NOTE ABOUT TEST SELECTION
FOR OLDER ADOLESCENTS

A question that practitioners often face is determining what test to select for administration when evaluating older adolescents. In particular, the MACI and MMPI–A have an upper age limit of 19 and 18 years, respectively, and the adult versions of these tests, the MCMI–III and MMPI–2, have lower age limits of 18 years. Therefore, the issue often arises with subjects who are 18 or 19 years of age as to whether the adult or adolescent version of the test should be selected.

The most practical strategy for resolving this question is to examine where the subject is developmentally by looking at his or her life circumstances. More specifically, if the older adolescent is living at home with parents, attending high school, and functioning in a more dependent capacity as do most teenagers, then the adolescent version of the test would be more appropriate. If, on the other hand, the individual is out of high school, living independently, has a job or attends college, and is functioning more like an autonomous adult, then the adult version of the test is more appropriate.

Other considerations include the clinical information provided by the test. For example, the MCMI−III has scales measuring severe personality disorders and clinical syndromes, whereas the MACI has scales addressing uniquely adolescent concerns. Test selection may depend on the specific type of clinical information that is needed. Selecting the right test depends more on clinical judgment in a given case than on the application of strict rules or guidelines, so long as the proper normative age range on each test is observed.

THE RORSCHACH

The Rorschach is a method for gathering information about an individual's personality functioning by presenting the subject with an ambiguous stimulus and requiring a specific response. In several ways, the Rorschach is very different from personality assessment methods that have been discussed so far in this text. Much of the controversy surrounding this instrument stems from the fact that it cannot be conceptualized as a single- or even multiple-scale personality instrument. As Weiner (1994) noted, the psychometric properties of reliability and validity must be evaluated in terms of the specific scores and indices on the Rorschach, not the overall instrument itself. Moreover, although many psychological assessment instruments are appropriately classified as tests, it has been suggested that the Rorschach may be best conceptualized not as a test but as a *technique* for generating information about an individual's perceptual, associational, affective, and other dynamic personality characteristics (Weiner, 1994).

Conceptualized as a perceptual−cognitive task, the Rorschach assesses the individual's abilities and preferences for processing the environment and responding in various situations. According to Exner (1993), Rorschach responses require visual input and encoding, classification of the stimulus, discarding of certain answers and responses, and selection of some response, based at times on personality traits and at other times on situational demands. Because the instrument was developed as a measure of intrapsychic processes, it was once thought to be impervious to faking, malingering, and other forms of response bias (Stermac, 1988). However, the issue of malingering and dissimulation on the Rorschach has been only modestly studied, and detection of dissimulation with the instrument among adolescent populations has not been formally explored.

Despite the lack of research on adolescent populations, there is still sufficient reason to examine the research that has been conducted on malingering and the Rorschach with adults. The basic reason for examining research on adult populations stands on the principle that "Rorschach behavior means what it means regardless of the age of the subject" (Exner & Weiner, 1982, p. 14). In other words, the interpretive significance of a given index or ratio on the Rorschach is the same for both adolescents and adults. For instance, poor form quality denotes perceptual inaccuracy or poor judgment in all populations. What is important with respect to age is the particular level at which an index or ratio becomes interpretively significant. Therefore, it is necessary when using the Rorschach in practice settings to use age-appropriate norms in order to determine at what level a particular Rorschach indicator is interpretable. More succinctly, the interpretive significance of various scores, determinants, responses, and the like remain the same in adult and adolescent populations. Research that does exist on the detection of deception with Rorschach results on adults can therefore inform use of the method with adolescents.

The research on dissimulation and the Rorschach has generally consisted of studies that are not sophisticated and that have several methodological weaknesses (Schretlen, 1988). In addition, Exner (1991) noted that an additional factor impeding the effectiveness of the Rorschach in detecting malingering and dissimulation is the fact that Rorschach data can reflect both long-term and situational factors in the individual's personality. Because malingering, denial, and other forms of deception are heavily dependent on situational factors, the examiner is often faced with the challenge of determining "if the product of the set is an integral part of the subject's psychological organization, or if it reflects an element that is transient or even incompatable with the basic personality structure or psychological functioning of the subject" (Exner, 1991, p. 428).

Detection of Denial and Positive Impression Management

One of the first attempts at examining the ability to detect faking of good impression was made by Carp and Shavzin (1950). Their results yielded inconsistent prediction of Rorschach variables that could be used to identify individuals who attempt to create a positive impression. With advances made in Rorschach scoring and analysis that were introduced by Exner's Comprehensive System (Exner, 1991, 1993), there have been more promising results. For instance, Seamons, Howell, Carlisle, and Roe (1981) found that individuals who were instructed to give responses on the Rorschach that would give an impression of psychological health or normality provide significantly more popular *(P)* responses, fewer stress-related determinants *(es)*, fewer inappropriate combinations *(FABCOM, INCOM)*, and thematic content that is less dramatic or sensational (e.g., blood, sex, aggression). The absence of many of these determinants is expected in well-adjusted respondents so that absence of these indicators is not specific to those respondents who are denying psychopathology. Thus, the use of these factors in isolation is not particularly instructive when screening for denial and minimization.

Another study on use of the Rorschach in evaluating denial and positive impression management was reported by Exner (1991). Rorschach protocols of 25 couples involved in child custody litigation were examined due to the greater motivation in this setting to appear healthy and well adjusted. The Rorschach indices associated significantly with attempts to simulate a positive impression were the Intellectualization Index *(2AB+ [Art+Ay])*, personalized *(PER)* scores, and popular *(P)* responses. Together, these indices reveal that individuals attempting to create a positive impression seek to appear more mature, sophisticated, and conventional. Additionally, individuals engaging in denial and positive impression management exhibit greater than average efforts at defending themselves and fending off challenges or perceived threat from others, as evidenced by high levels of personalized (PER) response content.

Based on this limited research, there are few firm conclusions that can be drawn on the utility of the Rorschach in detecting denial or the simulation of psychological health in adolescents. The fact that Rorschach indices and scores mean the same thing in adolescents and adults suggests that findings from this limited research apply to adolescents as well. Generally, the research suggests that attempts to appear psychologically well adjusted will yield Rorschach results that reflect responses to more obvious, conventional cues (P), an increased need to defend oneself against challenges (PER, Intellectualization Index), and fewer indices of bizarre or unusual content. Likewise, adolescents who are resistant, guarded, and hesitant to reveal much about themselves can be expected to provide a fewer number of responses (R) and higher levels of pure form (Lambda > .99). More important is the fact that these indices and scores are *suggestive* of denial and simulation of positive impressions. However, no clear cutoffs or decision rules have been formulated for specific Rorschach indices. According to Exner (1991), it may be difficult for an individual to simulate psychological health and adaptability unless he or she has some preexisting psychological strengths at his or her disposal. In other words, psychological difficulties or personality dysfunctions may have an impact on Rorschach performance, and an adolescent may compensate by reducing the amount of information a clinician has available (i.e., reduced R, increased Lambda) to make diagnostic decisions.

Rorschach indices associated with denial lack specificity, since they are found in populations other than those attempting to minimize or deny psychopathology. For example, a high number of popular (P) responses and an elevated Intellectualization Index may be expected in compulsive adolescents who are not necessarily situationally motivated to deny psychological problems. Given the unavailability of clear cutoffs, the best approach to interpreting Rorschach indices is by comparing an individual adolescent's scores and ratios against an appropriate normative sample (Exner & Weiner, 1982). Only in this manner is it then possible to make empirically based conclusions about the adolescent's Rorschach performance and his or her standing on a particular set of traits or characteristics. At this time, however, the best approach to using the Rorschach for evaluating denial and positive impression management is by using the data to support or disconfirm hypotheses derived from other aspects of the evaluation process.

Detection of Malingering and Negative Impression Management

Again, there is no research on malingering and the Rorschach pertaining to adolescent populations specifically, but research from adult populations is directly relevant because of the equivalent interpretative significance of Rorschach indices across all age groups (Exner & Weiner, 1982). There are many levels of sophistication among the studies on malingering on the Rorschach, with a range of interesting findings.

Given the large number of ratios and scores on Rorschach protocols, there has been a large degree of variability across studies. Some Rorschach measures have shown fairly consistent patterns across studies, whereas others have yielded inconclusive or unreliable patterns. The earliest investigation into the ability of respondents to change their performance on the Rorschach revealed that it is possible to do so (Feldman & Graley, 1954; Fosberg, 1938, 1941). However, it was not established whether an individual could effectively malinger psychosis, and few Rorschach indices yielded consistent results. These early studies have been criticized on methodological grounds in that respondents often took the Rorschach repeatedly under different instructional sets without the benefit of adequate control groups (Schretlen, 1988). Later studies have revealed that informed malingerers (i.e., respondents who are provided with information about characteristics of a particular illness) could not be distinguished from patients with genuine schizophrenia or psychosis (Albert, Fox, & Kahn, 1980). Bash and Alpert (1980) examined the effectiveness of a Malingering Index on the Rorschach for differentiating bona fide patients with paranoid schizophrenia from those who were suspected of feigning the illness. The Malingering Index consisted of 13 variables (i.e., R, Reaction Time, PSV, F-%, $FM+m$, $W{:}M$, $M{:}C$, W%, C%, P%, Rejections, AG, and failure to interpret easy plates). Although results yielded significantly higher elevations on the Malingering Index in the suspected feigners, it was not possible to identify the specific indices that contributed most to changes in Rorschach performance as a function of dissimulation.

A study by Seamons et al. (1981) used a test–retest design to examine whether or not malingerers provide an identifiable pattern of determinants with the Exner system. They administered the Rorschach to prison inmates from four diagnostic categories (nonschizophrenic, latent, residual, and psychotic schizophrenic) under two different instructional sets. In counterbalanced fashion, respondents were asked to appear "well adjusted" on one administration and then "mentally ill" on another administration. Results showed that there was no statistical difference between normal and malingered protocols. However, malingered protocols had significantly higher levels of dramatic content (e.g., blood, sex, fighting) and bizarre or inappropriate combinations (INCOM, FABCOM). The conclusions drawn by these researchers is that when form quality (i.e., $X+\%$ and $F+\%$) is in the normal range and there are higher than average levels of dramatic content and inappropriate combinations, there may be a greater likelihood of negative dissimulation.

These early studies of the ability to detect dissimulation on the Rorschach have produced conflicting results. However, those trends that have emerged with some recurring frequency are summarized in Exhibit 4.1. Several methodological issues have contributed to the lack of convincing findings on detecting dissimulation with the Rorschach. As Perry and Kinder (1990) noted, many researchers have found a reduction in R when respondents are asked to produce a Rorschach record that dissimulated in some direction. Similarly, there have been findings of a reduction in P, Lambda, Blends, and other indices when respondents are asked to provide a dissimulated Rorschach record. Perry and Kinder made the interesting observation that many Rorschach ratios, indices, and determinants are highly dependent on the productivity of the record and that reduction in R also reduces the range and frequency of various measures, resulting in experimental findings that are inconsistent and unreliable.

More recent attempts to identify common patterns of responding on the Rorschach among malingerers have used rather interesting procedures. Netter and Viglione (1994) examined the Rorschach responses of three groups of respondents: nonpatient controls, chronic schizophrenics, and nonpatients given instructions to malinger schizophrenia and who were offered an incentive to do so convincingly. One inter-

---

Exhibit 4.1
Rorschach Indices for Assessing Dissimulation

I. Denial/Minimization/Positive Impression Management
   A. Conventional responding: high *P*
   B. Defensiveness: high *(2AB+ [Art + Ay])*, high *PER*
   C. Restricted records: Low *R*, *Lambda* > 0.99, low Blends
   D. Absence of stress-related determinants: low *es (FM, m, Y, T, C', V)*
   E. Absence of sensationalistic content: low *Bl, Sx, AG, INCOM,* and *FABCOM*
II. Malingering/Symptom Exaggeration/Negative Impression Management
   A. Dramatic content: high *Bl, Sx, AG*, gore, mutilation, etc. (with good form quality as determined by *F+%* and *X+%*)
   B. High levels of *INCOM* and *FABCOM*
   C. Rejection of cards
   D. Restricted records: low *R*, low *P*
   E. Increased reaction time[a]

---

[a] Reaction time is no longer scored in the Exner Comprehensive System, so adequate norms are not available. Thus, this index is not recommended as a numerical index but may be useful as a general clinical observation.

esting finding is that some individuals in the malingering group were able to successfully fake schizophrenia on the Rorschach when provided with information on the illness. Netter and Viglione also found that "modified responses" on the Rorschach showed promise in the identification of malingering. Specifically, modified responses included the following: (a) evidence of a rambling, circumstantial response (i.e., *DR*) that either dramatizes a story or avoids the task of responding altogether; (b) personal comments about one's distress in the response (e.g., "This makes me crazy"); (c) creating an impression that the bizarre perception will come to life; (d) drawing attention to the bizarre nature of the response (e.g., "This is crazy-sounding, but . . ."); and (e) changing an initially good response to one that is of poor form quality or an inappropriate or fabulized combination. Thus, although some individuals are capable of effectively malingering schizophrenia when given adequate information about the condition, there also appear to be identifiable strategies that are employed by malingerers when faking schizophrenia.

One major drawback of the methodology used in the Netter and Viglione (1994) study is that it involves the use of a respondent group that is asked to simulate malingering according to a particular set of instructions. This research strategy results in a more readily obtainable experimental group of malingerers but fails to represent some of the strategies employed by malingerers in actual clinical practice. Ganellen, Wasyliw, Haywood, and Grossman (1996) examined the ability to detect malingering on the Rorschach in forensic patients charged with serious crimes who were assigned to one of two groups (i.e., honest and malingering) based on their scores on MMPI validity scales. Respondents in the malingering group could not be differentiated from the honest group based on Exner Comprehensive System variables, but malingerers did provide significantly more dramatic responses (e.g., blood). Although these researchers suggested that combination of the MMPI and Rorschach is more powerful than the Rorschach alone in detecting malingering, there are some difficulties with experimentally classifying forensic patients as malingerers or as honest respondents based on MMPI scores alone. Although the prevalence of malingering would be expected to be greater, there are undoubtedly false positives and false negatives that are included in the malingering and honest groups, respectively. Still, these results provide additional support for the validity of Rorschach responses with dramatic content as an indication of potential malingering; however, no single Rorschach index or ratio is definitive evidence of dissimulation. The recommendation made by Ganellen and his colleagues to combine different measures of malingering with one another appears to be a sound one and can be extended to adolescent evaluations by combining the MMPI–A, MACI, and/or SIRS with Rorschach records when assessing dissimulation in adolescents.

Few studies have looked at the ability of the Rorschach to detect malingering of disturbances other than psychosis. However, Frueh and Kinder (1994) examined the ability of individuals to malinger combat-related posttraumatic stress disorder (PTSD). Although there is little relevance of combat-related PTSD to adolescent populations, the findings from this investigation support trends established with other studies. In particular, malingerers provided Rorschach responses that were overly dramatic, less complex, showed evidence of weaker emotional controls in responses, and revealed exaggerated impairment in reality testing.

In summary, there are no studies examining sensitivity of the Rorschach to detect malingering in adolescents. However, research on adult populations has direct relevance to teenagers, because Rorschach ratios, indices, and determinants have the same interpretive meaning in both adolescent and adult populations. None of the studies conducted on dissimulation and the Rorschach have established operating characteristics such as positive or negative predictive power. Presently, there are only trends and specific patterns of responding that can be useful in establishing whether or not a given respondent is dissimulating. Exhibit 4.1 outlines the Rorschach indices that can be used in assisting with diagnostic decision making.

NEUROPSYCHOLOGICAL AND INTELLECTUAL TESTING

In recent years there has been increased interest in the ability to detect feigned neuropsychological deficits on standardized psychological tests. What makes the detection of dissimulation of cognitive impairment different from feigned psychopathology is that the former involves denial of abilities that are normally present in the individual, whereas the latter involves production or exaggeration of symptoms that are not typically present (Rogers, Harrell, & Liff, 1993). In other words, malingering of neuropsychological deficits involves the denial of cognitive abilities, whereas malingering of psychopathology involves the intentional fabrication of symptoms. For this reason, Rogers and his colleagues have called for a different set of strategies and conceptual framework for developing effective methods of detecting malingering in neuropsychological assessment.

One of the major obstacles to detecting malingering in neuropsychological assessment is that there is a relative paucity of research on this topic (Franzen, Iverson, & McCracken, 1990; Rogers, Harrell, & Liff, 1993). There are no well-validated standards and guidelines that have been established to detect faking on many standard neuropsychological tests (Cullum, Heaton, & Grant, 1991). Moreover, there are no studies on adolescent populations in terms of their performance on instruments under "honest" and malingering conditions. A series of studies by Faust and his colleagues, although not testing the differential patterns of bona fide patients and malingerers, is directly relevant to the issue of malingering in adolescents. In each of these studies, children (Faust, Hart, & Guilmette, 1988) and adolescents (Faust, Hart, Guilmette, & Arkes, 1988) were instructed to fake poor neuropsychological test results, and the resultant protocols were submitted to clinical neuropsychologists for analysis. Results from these studies showed that experts in the field of neuropsychology were unable to detect feigning or malingering in the record, suggesting that children and adolescents can effectively fake believable neuropsychological deficits without detection.

There have been legitimate criticisms made of the Faust et al. studies, including the fact that blind interpretation of test scores is a highly questionable practice (Bigler, 1990). Moreover, these studies involved experts who did not have much of the material that is crucial for identifying feigning, namely collateral reports, medical records, clinical observations, and other relevant documents (Schmidt, 1989). However, despite these methodological limitations, the experts in Faust's studies still rated the confidence they had in their judgments as high. More than anything else, this series of studies reveals that an area of psychological assessment often held to be more objective and scientifically based than others has not escaped the limitations inherent in attempting to uncover feigned psychological difficulties.

There are six strategies for identifying potential malingering in neuropsychological assessment that have been identified by Rogers, Harrell, and Liff (1993). The first of these strategies is *floor effect*, in which participants are given tasks in which severely impaired individuals are expected to succeed. Evidence of impairment on these relatively simple tasks (e.g., "Tell me your name") is taken as a sign of malingering or feigning. A second detection strategy is *performance curve*, in which participants are presented with a series of tasks that are arranged from very easy to increasingly more difficult. This model forms the basis for arrangement of items on many psychoeducational tests such as the *Wechsler Intelligence Scale for Children–Third Edition* (WISC–III; Wechsler, 1991). A performance curve strategy operates under the assumption that individuals with genuine cognitive impairment will reach the level of their capabilities and begin failing more difficult items, whereas malingerers will instead show inconsistent and spotty performance on increasingly more difficult tasks. The third detection strategy identified by Rogers and his colleagues is *magnitude of error*, in which specific features of the incorrect responses of malingerers are compared with those of patients with genuine neuropsychological impairment; in particular, the patterns of approximate but incorrect and grossly wrong answers (e.g., Ganser syndrome) are compared between groups of dissimulators and patients. *Symptom validity testing* is the fourth neuropsychological dissimulation detection strategy. Under this paradigm, individuals claiming a deficit are provided with a large number of trials for a task in which they are to select between two alternatives (e.g., presence or absence of a tactile sensation while blindfolded). Accordingly, individuals with a genuine deficit are expected to have a 50% error rate by chance when the stimulus is randomly administered 50% of the time; malingerers are expected to have an error rate below chance level (e.g., 10% correct) because they are deliberately selecting the response. The fifth detection strategy is *atypical presentation*, in which a participant's performance is considered to be indicative of malingering when there is evidence of inconsistent performance across repeated administrations of the testing or unusual performance patterns that are not consistent with established patterns among individuals with known neurological impairment. Finally, Rogers and his colleagues outlined a sixth strategy for identifying malingering on neuropsychological testing as being *psychological sequelae*. Under this approach, malingering is suspected when participants report an unusually high number of psychological symptoms.

Of the six strategies discussed, only a few have been tested empirically, including floor effect, performance curve, and symptom validity testing (Rogers, Harrell, & Liff, 1993). Moreover, some of the strategies are of questionable utility because there has been little empirical research on their validity. A few of these strategies, such as atypical presentation, have limited clinical utility because some genuinely neurologically impaired participants have inconsistent or unusual presentations on testing (Pankratz, 1988).

There are two approaches used to investigate patterns of testing performance that can help to identify adolescent malingerers on neuropsychological tests. One is to evaluate the performance of adolescents on tests designed specifically for this population under controlled conditions. Thus, neuropsychological instruments for adolescents are administered to groups of control individuals under honest conditions, suspected juvenile malingerers, and groups of adolescents instructed to feign cognitive impairment; the results are analyzed to see if different patterns emerge to assist in classification. Unfortunately, what limited research of this type exists has been conducted on adults; there is no controlled research on adolescent populations.

A second research approach to identifying malingering in adolescents is to survey research on neuropsychological instruments that are used in adult populations but that have adolescent norms, thus permitting applications of these tests to adolescent populations. One example of such an instrument is the Luria Nebraska Neuropsychological Battery (LNNB; Golden, Hammeke, & Purisch, 1980). Age norms for the LNNB are low enough to include adolescents age 15 years and up. There is one study (Mensch & Woods, 1986) that has examined patterns of feigned brain injury on the LNNB. Although this study examined adults age 24 to 46, the findings have some relevance to adolescents because norms for the LNNB go down to the adolescent years. Mensch and Woods administered the LNNB to two groups of participants, one of average intelligence and the other of above average intelligence. The

Table 4.5

Criteria for Suspected Feigning on the Bender Visual Motor Gestalt Test

Criterion	Definition
1. Inhibited Figure Size	Each figure that can be covered by a 3.2 cm square is scored +1.
2. Changed Position	Rotation on easily recognized figure more than 45° is scored +1.
3. Distorted Relationship	Easily recognized figure that has parts correctly drawn but relationships misplaced is scored +1.
4. Complex Additions	Easily recognized figures given an additional bizarre or complex detail is scored +1.
5. Gross Simplification	Each figure with a developmental level of 6 years or less is scored +1.
6. Inconsistent Form Quality	Protocol containing a figure with a developmental level of 6 years or less and one with a level of 9 years or more is scored +1.

on the Wechsler Intelligence Scales. Although research has focused on the adult version of these tests, the Wechsler Adult Intelligence Scale–Revised (WAIS–R), many of the findings have direct relevance to the WISC–III because of the underlying unifying theory of intelligence that forms the basis for each instrument and the parallel subtests and administration formats that exist for the WAIS–R and the WISC–III. In addition, the WAIS–R has norms that go down to age 16, making it an instrument suited for evaluations of older adolescents. Therefore, research on feigning with the Wechsler Intelligence Scales may have implications also for identifying feigning in adolescent populations.

Several studies have shown that Digit Span is particularly useful in distinguishing feigners from psychiatric patients in that feigners show poorer performance on both digits forward and reverse (Heaton, Smith, Lehman, & Vogt, 1978; Rawling & Brooks, 1990). The study by Rawling and Brooks also suggests that haphazard sequencing errors on Picture Arrangement should raise suspicions about possible feigning of head injury. Also, errors on the Arithmetic subtest involving Ganser-type symptoms in which the individual gives incorrect answers that are "one off" the correct response or approximate answers should raise suspicions about possible feigning. Compared to a group of patients with bona fide symptoms of head injury, individuals with only mild head injury who were believed to be feigning more severe deficits were found to perform significantly better on Picture Completion and Object Assembly, whereas their performance was poorer on Arithmetic, Comprehension, Picture Arrangement, and Block Design.

The assessment of malingering and deception in neuropsychological evaluation is one of the more rapidly growing areas of research and clinical interest. This trend is spurred in large measure by the increasing relevance of neuropsychology in evaluations of criminal defendants and civil litigants in personal injury cases. Although some of the research produced thus far can help to guide evaluations, there remains a great need for more research on adolescent populations.

CONCLUSION

The use of standardized psychological testing is a key component in any psychological evaluation where there is a suspicion of malingering or deception. Although the use of these instruments in forensic settings is crucial, the relative ease with which some instruments, particularly self-report tests, can be used makes clinical applications highly practical. Moreover, there is a growing research base on the use of psychological tests to evaluate malingering, but this application in adolescent populations is not extensive. More research is needed.

In this chapter, I have shown how established instruments such as the MMPI–A and Rorschach can be particularly useful, and the more recent MACI holds considerable promise. Each of these instruments serves as one component in a comprehensive assessment. The assessment of malingering in neuropsychological evaluation is based on explicit theoretical principles, but the research again focuses primarily on adults, and there remains a significant need for research on adolescents.

Overall, psychological testing contributes an important part to an evaluation, and there is no single instrument or test indicator that provides definitive evidence of malingering or deception. Instead, test results are useful as corroborative data to help support or reject hypotheses formulated during the course of a comprehensive evaluation. The most judicious use of psychological testing is one that integrates the results with findings from the individual's history, clinical interview, and evaluation of contextual factors.

5

Professional, Legal, and Ethical Issues

Formulating a diagnosis in clinical assessment is one of the many components of a comprehensive psychological assessment. It is not just labeling or classifying symptoms that is important, but evaluating etiology, symptom severity, and the course of a disorder that are among the most crucial facets of assessment. In most cases, a clinician renders a diagnosis with the ultimate goal being effective treatment of the patient's symptoms to reduce suffering or improve functioning. When dealing with matters involving potential malingering or dissimulation, the treatment-oriented approach to assessment does not easily apply. Among the many reasons for this state of affairs is the implicit assumption by many individuals, trained and untrained alike, that malingerers, feigners, or others who dissemble clinical symptoms are "fakers" who are liars that should be cast aside in favor of those who are more "worthy" of treatment and other valuable resources. Although this is sometimes true, not all malingerers are best served by such harsh treatment.

As with many diagnostic challenges in clinical practice, matters are not as clear-cut as simply making the determination that someone is or is not feigning. Clearly, there are those that fall at each of these extremes; however, there are also those who fall somewhere in between. For example, symptom exaggeration or factitious disorders involve a degree of feigning or deception, but the symptomatology of these disturbances frequently represents a manifestation of more pervasive psychopathology that is genuine and in need of treatment. In the same way, determination of the validity of an individual's manifestation of psychopathology in legal settings is not simple or straightforward. Many times, the proper administration of justice depends on the accuracy and validity of a clinician's findings as to whether or not a given defendant is dissimulating.

Because of the many factors influencing the nature and degree of dissimulation an adolescent displays, as well as the ramifications of rendering a diagnosis or opinion on the veracity of an adolescent's self-reports, it is important to recognize that many professional, ethical, scientific, and legal issues arise in assessments on adolescent dissimulation. Clinicians cannot ignore these issues if the goal is to provide high-quality services. One must make sure that opinions and conclusions are used appropriately and are based on sound theoretical and scientific principles. In the remainder of this volume, a variety of these issues will be discussed. In this chapter, I explore several important legal, ethical, and professional concerns. These issues include a review of research on the accuracy of professionals in detecting dissimulation, ethical issues in diagnosing malingering, admissibility of expert opinion, and standards for selecting tests and instruments used to detect dissimulation. By addressing these issues, it is hoped that assessments on adolescent malingering and deception will be conducted appropriately and ethically and that clinicians will be diligent in conducting thorough, ethical, and scientifically sound evaluations on adolescent dissimulation.

THE ABILITY OF PROFESSIONALS TO DETECT MALINGERING

Recall from chapter 4 that in studies on the ability of professionals to detect malingering, questions have been raised as to whether or not clinicians can do so effectively. Studies by Faust and his colleagues (Faust, Hart, & Guilmette, 1988; Faust, Hart, Guilmette, & Asher, 1988) examined the ability of experienced neuropsychologists to detect malingering in test protocols of children and adolescents who took a battery of neuropsychological tests either under normal conditions or with instructions to deliberately feign neurological injury. These studies revealed that experts were unable to detect malingering in the records, and younger participants were held to be capable of faking believable impairment without detection. Although there is scant research in this area, recent findings cast doubt on the inability of psychologists to detect malingering.

Bigler (1990) criticized the findings of Faust and his colleagues on methodological grounds by stating that the practice of blindly interpreting neuropsychological test results without sufficient background information is highly suspect and does not reflect proper clinical practice. Schmidt (1989) added that insufficient access to other materials such as medical records or collateral reports contributed to the weak findings. An additional criticism of findings from the Faust studies is that they focus on the ability of clinicians to detect malingering through a form of psychological assessment (i.e., neuropsychological testing) on a population (i.e., children and adolescents) that has little or no formal empirical research on particular measures or techniques. Therefore, there is no empirical research base on which to draw when attempting to identify malingering.

Recently, these criticisms of methodology used in the studies by Faust and his colleagues have been tested empirically by Bourg, Connor, and Landis (1995). These researchers asked a group of diplomates in forensic psychology and a group of general clinical psychologists to review assessment data from one of four types of cases. Professionals from these two groups reviewed a case in which the individual was either a diagnosed malingerer or a person acquitted by reason of insanity. The psychologists were able to identify malingering with an accuracy rate of 86.4%. What makes this result an improvement over the success rate cited by Faust and his colleagues is that researchers provided several pieces of information, thus making more extensive information available to forensic practitioners. This approach more closely reflects actual practice situations. Moreover, real as opposed to simulated malingerers participated in the experimental group. Therefore, the study by Bourg and colleagues has good external validity and generalizes to the area of standard forensic practice. It is of interest, however, that the study revealed no difference between diplomates and general clinicians in their ability to detect malingering, casting doubt on the notion that experience has any connection to one's level of accuracy in identifying malingering. In other words, it appears that the quality and thoroughness of one's work has more to do with its adequacy than the specific credentials or experience one has.

Another recent study by Trueblood and Binder (1997) demonstrated that neuropsychological and cognitive impairment can be distinguished from malingering fairly well by psychologists. In this study, neuropsychological testing protocols from clinical malingerers (i.e., individuals deemed to be malingering in an actual clinical setting) and individuals with bona fide traumatic brain injury were sent to psychologists who were then asked a series of questions about diagnosis, the likelihood of malingering, and the level of confidence in one's ratings. The rate of error for detecting malingering (i.e., identifying those who were malingering as being head injured) averaged about 10% across the malingering cases. On the other hand, 92% of psychologists correctly identified head-injured subjects. These researchers cautioned against generalizing their results, however, because it is unclear what strategies psychologists used in their analyses. However, this study has some strengths in that it tested actual clinical, as opposed to simulated, malingerers and provided clinicians with contextual information that raised the appropriate level of concern that malingering was suspected.

The methodology used in studies of the ability of professionals to detect malingering is a very important factor. When limited data are provided to a clinician and the true level of motivation of the participant to dissimulate is unknown or suspect, results are not generalizable to actual practice. More recent research suggests that with improved methodology, where data provided to professionals are richer and the motivation of participants to malinger is similar to that of a "true malingerer," then the capacity of professionals to detect malingering is better than it was once thought to be. However, more research is needed to explore the strategies used by clinicians to detect malingering in actual practice.

THE ETHICS OF DIAGNOSING MALINGERING

A recent case in which I was asked to perform a forensic psychological evaluation illustrates very well that practitioners not only must conduct a careful and detailed assessment of the adolescent suspected of malingering, but also must remain sensitive to how the diagnosis of malingering can impact subsequent treatment and disposition of the adolescent. The case involved an individual named Randy who had been charged with aggravated assault on a corrections officer following a confrontation in court, where the teenager had been sentenced to 10 days in jail on an unrelated harassment charge. At the time of sentencing, the judge directed the officer to take Randy into custody. A physical altercation ensued from a brief but heated exchange after Randy demanded to go outside briefly to see his girlfriend. Thinking Randy was about to escape, the corrections officer physically restrained him when Randy ignored the officer's verbal warning and turned to go outside the building. Of the many issues to be determined in the evaluation, one was Randy's capacity to form the intent to prevent the corrections officer from performing his lawful duty, a key element of the crime.

The history revealed a long pattern of disruptive, oppositional, and violent behavior. Randy had been treated for hyperactivity as a youth, and he had been hospitalized four times in psychiatric facilities for suicidal gestures, aggressive defiance at home, and other conduct disturbances. His history also revealed three prior head injuries of a very serious nature, one which had resulted in a fractured skull approximately 3 years earlier. As a child, he had been rendered unconscious by a severe electrical shock, and he had an abnormal EEG in which temporal/frontal-lobe abnormalities were noted. In addition to the neurological condition indicated by these findings, Randy had a lengthy history of very heavy substance abuse, including heavy cocaine, marijuana, LSD, amphetamine, and narcotics abuse. At various times he had been diagnosed with an organic personality disorder, APD, and polysubstance dependence.

Immediately after his arrest on the recent charge of aggravated assault, he was found to be incompetent to stand trial by two forensic examiners and sent to a forensic mental hospital for restoration of his fitness to proceed. The hospital record indicated an admission diagnosis of adjustment disorder with mixed disturbance of emotions and conduct and polysubstance dependence, with diagnoses of organic mental disorder and antisocial personality disorder to be ruled out. During the course of hospitalization, no psychological testing was conducted, and neurological testing was not performed until 2 days before Randy was discharged back to the county jail after being found fit to proceed; no formal neurologist's report had been written on the test results. However, the hospital staff obtained collateral information from the two examiners who had found him to be incompetent and from a community mental health worker who consulted at the jail where he had originally been incarcerated. Apparently, Randy was "well known" to the staff at the county jail and community mental health center. Hospital records clearly documented that he was seen by the community mental health worker as a "manipulator" who was a severe substance abuser seeking treatment only to obtain prescription medications. Within days of the conversation with the mental health worker, the hospital staff discussed the case, and the diagnosis was suddenly changed to malingering, polysubstance dependence, and APD. Randy was taken off all medications, which, according to records that were later obtained from prior treating psychiatrists, were an anticonvulsant (for emotional lability related to a seizure disorder) and a narcotic (for severe and continuous headaches). The worsening of his symptoms following withdrawal of all medications was attributed to malingering.

Regardless of the propriety of using medications with abuse potential (i.e., narcotics) in a patient having a severe substance abuse history, the diagnosis of malingering in this case had profound and adverse consequences. When Randy was evaluated, he had not received any medication from the jail medical staff for 2 months. His headaches had intensified and they were reported to be continuous. His affect was extremely labile and he had problems with dizziness and visual impairment. Subsequent testing revealed clear neuropsychological deficits in a pattern consistent with his head injuries, although his chronic substance abuse undoubtedly clouded the results. Additional psychological testing revealed symptom exaggeration, but none of the tests were invalid or rose to the level of deliberate feigning; he was expressing numerous symptoms and reporting high levels of psychopathology that were supported by his history and clinical presentation.

This case illustrates how a patient's reputation, stereotypes of forensic patients as malingerers, and other negative biases can have a detrimental impact on the validity of a patient's diagnosis and the subsequent treatment plan implemented. Moreover, a diagnosis of malingering may be difficult for a patient to shed, and treatment may be forever affected in an adverse manner. On the other hand, failure to identify an adolescent who is malingering or in other ways distorting his or her symptom presentation may lead to improper treatment of that adolescent, admission for services when no treatment may be required, and other negative outcomes. In short, the practice of making diagnostic assessments on adolescent malingering and deception can have profound effects on the type of treatment an adolescent receives. Therefore, such assessments should be conducted in an ethical, professional, and detailed manner.

As just demonstrated, there are potential risks in making a diagnosis of malingering in adolescents, just as there are in failing to make the diagnosis when strong evidence indicates its presence. Of more direct concern to the practitioner, however, is the risk of a malpractice suit brought on behalf of the adolescent for misdiagnosis if the teenager or his family believes that the alleged psychopathology is bona fide and not the product of malingering. For some practitioners, these risks may be sufficient to lead them to avoid rendering conclusions in cases where malingering is an issue. This approach is a bit extreme, but the issue of potential liability does underline the fact that assessments in this area should not be taken lightly and that a thorough evaluation is indicated. The approach advocated here is not to avoid assessments of malingering altogether but rather to undertake them using adequate information, good clinical judgment, and a diligent adherence to professional ethics.

Several professional standards exist that guide psychological practice. Of course, there are the "Ethical Principles of Psychologists and Code of Conduct" (APA, 1992). For psychologists practicing in forensic contexts, there are the *Specialty Guidelines for Forensic Psychologists* published by Division 41 of the APA (Committee on Ethical Guidelines for Forensic Psychologists, 1991). Both of these professional standards are useful in directing ethical assessment of adolescents where malingering is a key issue.

The APA Ethical Principles generally require that psychologists be competent (Principle A) in their area of practice and that their evaluations maintain integrity (Principle B) and respect for people's rights and dignity (Principle D). Therefore, when undertaking evaluations on an adolescent's potential for dissimulation, the psychologist should be familiar with adolescent development, research on lying and deception in children and adolescents, and the various assessment techniques available for evaluating adolescent personality and psychopathology. Assessments on adolescent malingering should be based also on scientific and empirical methods rather than on vague clinical conjecture or mere speculation (Principle C). One should also remain aware of the impact one's conclusions may have on how that adolescent is treated by other professionals, the criminal justice system, and other agencies (Principles E and F).

There is no one ethical principle or standard in the APA code that guides practice in cases where dissimulation is a relevant concern. However, a few of the standards are important. All opinions and conclusions on adolescent malingering and dissimulation should be based on sound scientific and professional models (Standard 1.06), not collateral opinions from biased observers as illustrated in Randy's case at the beginning of this section. Practitioners may be better off clarifying terms and concepts and avoiding the use of pejorative terms such as *faking, ma-*

nipulator, or *liar* in favor of more appropriate terms such as *symptom overreporting, minimization,* or *dissimulation,* because the latter terms avoid stereotyping the subject. Moreover, less pejorative terms make it easier to explain the dynamics of a given case in clear and understandable terms, particularly to lay jurors, case workers, judges, and attorneys. Psychologists must assure that the findings from their evaluations are not misused, including any diagnoses or labels they may apply (Standards 1.15 and 1.16).

A particularly sensitive ethical issue arises when psychologists are asked by a third party (typically via a court order or request from an attorney) to conduct an evaluation on an individual (Standards 1.20 and 1.21). The need for informed consent in these circumstances is also recognized in the *Specialty Guidelines for Forensic Psychologists* (see Section IV.E.). The psychologist performing a forensic evaluation must provide the subject with notification of the purpose, methods, and intended uses of the findings from the evaluation. Suppose that an evaluation is being conducted of a juvenile accused of a crime, and a question about insanity or criminal responsibility is asked. Is the psychologist required to tell the adolescent that his or her mental state at the time of evaluation is being determined? The answer to this question is affirmative, but the interesting issue becomes whether or not the psychologist is also required to inform the adolescent that the veracity of his or her self-reports will be evaluated and that psychological tests will be used to assist in determining if any claims of psychopathology are feigned. Clearly, more detailed information will more than satisfy the requirement for obtaining informed consent, but the evaluation will be compromised by putting the adolescent in a position of filtering self-reports or slanting information in the direction of providing the "best answers" to create a desired impression. The genuine symptom picture may thus be distorted.

Even more important is whether or not the adolescent must be informed that the possible intended use of the findings of an evaluation is to refuse services if the adolescent is found to be malingering in treatment setting evaluations. Such a detailed informed consent notice may create the impression of the evaluator as an adversary or opponent, further disrupting some of the rapport needed to complete a proper psychological evaluation.

One response to these dilemmas is to outline an informed consent that is ethically and sufficiently detailed, while also providing an appropriate level of restraint. To this end, it is entirely appropriate to inform the adolescent that the purpose of the evaluation is to evaluate his or her mental state, or some other psychological status. Because the findings are at that point unknown, the results may be supportive of the defendant's case or they may not be. If the psychologist is working for the defense, the findings will be reported to the attorney and he or she will decide how the opinion is to be used legally (i.e., either to have the psychologist testify or not to use the psychologist's opinion). When operating as a court-appointed expert, the psychologist must inform the adolescent that the findings will be reported back to the court and that all parties, at the judge's discretion, will have access to the results. This strategy provides information about how the results may be used but does not go into unnecessary detail about the issues of malingering, feigning, and so forth. When obtaining informed consent in clinical treatment settings, the psychologist should also inform the adolescent that the results may be used to determine the treatment plan that will be developed, if that is the purpose of the evaluation. The psychologist will then need to be sure that the final opinion and results are used in an ethical manner as noted earlier. This approach will avoid unnecessary contamination of both the assessment setting and the subject's approach to the evaluation.

The assessment of dissimulation relies to a large extent on the use of psychological testing instruments. As the discussion in the previous two chapters illustrates, standardized psychological assessment instruments are invaluable for answering specific questions about an adolescent's response style. Therefore, general ethical standards pertaining to the use of psychological tests are particularly important when evaluating adolescent dissimulation. In particular, psychologists should be competent in the appropriate administration and interpretation of psychological assessment instruments (Standard 2.02) and should be well versed in the use of instruments that are appropriate to adolescents

(Standard 2.04). The materials in previous chapters have been written to help practitioners meet this latter requirement. One very important standard of practice that has direct bearing on evaluations involving dissimulation is the proper maintenance of test security (Standard 2.10). Psychologists are required to keep proper records and to make available to the courts all data and information that provide the foundation for testimony and rendered opinions (see Standards 5.04 and 7.02; see also *Specialty Guidelines* VI.B.). When disclosure of psychological test protocols is required, the psychologist should maintain proper test security by obtaining a court order listing the materials to be disclosed and the name of the psychologist for the opposing side who will interpret the records. Proper test security dictates that raw test scores and scoring algorithms not be disclosed to nonpsychological professionals. Generally, an appeal to the presiding judge and, if necessary, presenting a copy of the APA Ethical Principles and Specialty Guidelines have typically been found to be sufficient for resolving any conflicts between ethical standards and legal disclosure requirements in these matters.

The diagnosis of malingering or other forms of dissimulation in adolescents can have profound and lasting effects on the subsequent treatment or legal disposition for a given adolescent. As a general rule, therefore, when rendering opinions or writing reports that address issues of reliability and validity of an adolescent's self-reports, conclusions should be provided only when doing so is relevant and can be justified and substantiated on the basis of sound data. For example, an adolescent is examined with respect to competence to stand trial, and the assessment results give clear evidence that the defendant understands the legal proceedings and charges and can assist with the defense. Statements that are made as to the likelihood of malingering or dissimulation if an insanity defense were to be raised would not be appropriate, because this issue does not bear directly on the adolescent's capacity to stand trial. However, the teenager's ability to at least appraise the feasibility of such a potential defense would be relevant to his or her competence to stand trial. Likewise, conclusions about the juvenile's possible malingering would not be appropriate if the opinion were based solely on one interview and without collateral information or psychological testing of the teenager. Direct clinical observations, psychological testing, clinical interviews with the defendant, and records should also be used when formulating an opinion.

It is also recommended that when rendering opinions or writing reports, one should make statements in a tasteful, professional, and clear manner. Conclusory opinions such as, "The defendant is lying" or "This youth is manipulating to avoid punishment" have a slanted tone and can bias the reader. Moreover, they provide little insight into why the conclusion is made. On the other hand, instructive statements such as the following may be more illuminating for the reader: "This youth, while overreporting the level of symptoms typically found in adolescent populations, is still experiencing some bona fide difficulties."

Sometimes it is also necessary to qualify at what point in time an adolescent is dissimulating. For example, one forensic evaluation revealed that the defendant in a murder case was providing inconsistent and exaggerated self-reports of pathology. However, this occurred after he had been incarcerated for several months while awaiting trial and had been receiving psychotropic medication. At the time of the murder, he had not been taking medication, despite a history of several hospitalizations for acute paranoid psychosis. A videotaped interview by police officers, within an hour of the crime, provided rich data on his mental state very near the time of the killing. In addressing the issue of malingering, a distinction had to be drawn in the report between the bona fide symptoms of a psychotic individual at the time of the offense and the dissimulated and unreliable self-reports of that same person who was now stabilized on medication and having to answer for a horrible crime. The distinction was important in the determination of his mental state at the time of offense.

ADMISSIBILITY OF EVIDENCE

When mental health professionals conduct evaluations on individuals involved in some legal proceeding, there is a strong likelihood that the results from that assessment will be presented at a court hearing or trial. It is therefore helpful to have some appreciation for the legal standards used to evaluate the admissibility of the testimony and for providing results from one's evaluation in a coherent and organized manner. The following material provides the potential expert witness with guidelines to consider when testifying in court.

General Issues Concerning Expert Testimony

In legal settings, the job of the trier of fact (i.e., judge or jury) is to decide on ultimate legal issues such as the guilt or innocence of a defendant, what the monetary amount of damages is, and whether or not a party's request should be granted (e.g., custody of a child). This decision-making process is carried out by weighing the amount of evidence presented, evaluating the strength or credibility of witnesses, and applying the evidence to standards outlined by the law. A major form of evidence in legal settings is the expert testimony of mental health professionals. Expert testimony is usually offered in the form of opinion based on some formal method of data collection and analysis. As I will show shortly, experts are unlike fact witnesses who give testimony based on their perceptions of an event or set of circumstances, because experts are permitted to offer opinions based on knowledge and experience that is assumed to be beyond the realm of expertise attributed to the typical juror. Thus, expert testimony is generally viewed as being grounded in a theoretical and scientific discipline that can assist the trier of fact when reaching a decision in legal settings.

Mental health professionals who evaluate juveniles in legal contexts must address issues related to the credibility and reliability of self-reports because of the greater concern over feigning and dissimulation in forensic settings. Invariably, mental health experts who testify in court about the findings from adolescent psychological evaluations are questioned strongly under cross-examination with such questions as: "So, Doctor, you really are relying only on what the defendant told you, aren't you?" If the expert approaches the assessment of an adolescent's credibility with a broad-based, multimethod approach, then the expert can base his or her opinion on more than just unconfirmed self-reports of the teenager. The use of standardized psychological tests and instruments permit the examiner to ground expert opinion in scientific and empirical principles rather than unsubstantiated speculations. Likewise, the use of collateral records and informants permits verification of information obtained during clinical interviews.

The legal standards that determine whether or not an expert witness will be allowed to render an opinion in a legal case on any issue, let alone the adolescent's credibility, are outlined by rules of evidence. Evidentiary rules differ among various state and federal jurisdictions, so experts need to be familiar with the particular rules in the jurisdiction in which testimony is offered. Some states, such as New York, have common-law rules of evidence that are the product of a long line of cases, whereas other states have codified their rules of evidence in the form of statutory law. The admissibility of evidence in federal courts is determined by the *Federal Rules of Evidence* (FRE; 1992); in addition, the FRE have served as a model for evidentiary rules in many states.

A major reason for the need to be cognizant of evidentiary standards is that certain testimony may not be allowed unless it meets the requirements of admissibility under the particular rules of evidence in effect. Therefore, one can assist in preparing testimony for presentation in court by being familiar with proper rules of evidence. There are two general standards or legal tests that form the basis for admissibility of expert testimony in most jurisdictions, the FRE and the standard outlined in *United States v. Frye* (1923), commonly known as the *Frye* test. More recently, the United States Supreme Court ruling in *Daubert v. Merrill Dow Pharmaceuticals* (1993) has strengthened application of the FRE in federal courts.

The *Frye* test has been adopted by many state courts (e.g., New York, Florida) and has been referred to as the "general acceptance" test. Accordingly, for expert testimony to be admissible, it must be established to such a degree that the substantive nature of the testimony has achieved general acceptance in the field to which it belongs. Although many issues about the assessment of malingering and deception are unresolved, there is a body of research, much of which is cited in the references in this volume, that outlines a number of techniques and strategies used in the assessment of self-report accuracy. Moreover, response style evaluations are a crucial part of standard forensic psychological assessment (Heilbrun, 1992; Rogers, 1988a). Therefore, the general acceptance of this body of research can be readily established.

The *Frye* test was once the standard test for admissibility of evidence in federal and most state courts. However, state and federal evidentiary laws are different. In 1993, the United States Supreme Court ruling in *Daubert v. Merrill Dow Pharmaceuticals* explicitly rejected the *Frye* test in federal court by ruling that the purpose of the FRE is to guide admissibility of evidence in federal courts. However, the *Frye* standard of general acceptance is identified in the *Daubert* decision as one of many factors that judges should consider when determining the admissibility of evidence. Consequently, all federal courts adopt the FRE, whereas state courts adopt either the state evidentiary code (sometimes modeled after the FRE) or state common law. Some states, such as Florida and New York, have explicitly retained the *Frye* test even in light of the *Daubert* ruling, whereas others have continued to use the *Frye* test without explicit ruling.

The FRE require that for evidence to be admissible, it must be relevant (Rule 402), which means that evidence is relevant if it has the "tendency to make the existence of any fact that is of consequence to the determination of the action more probable or less probable than it would be without the evidence" (Rule 401). However, many forms of evidence are highly relevant to the determination of a legal issue, but they are never admitted into evidence. The reason for exclusion of certain types of evidence is that the "probative value" may be outweighed by unfair prejudice to the defendant, or it may be confusing, misleading, or contribute to undue delay (Rule 403). Therefore, evidence must not only be relevant, but it must also be highly probative and minimally prejudicial, costly, and confusing.

The FRE also permit experts to render opinions "if scientific, technical, or other specialized knowledge will assist the trier of fact to understand the evidence or to determine a fact in issue" (Rule 702). In simplified terms, the FRE have been construed as advancing a "helpfulness" standard for admissibility of evidence, and they are often seen as more liberal and less restrictive than the *Frye* test's general acceptance requirement. With respect to opinion on an adolescent's propensity to malinger or engage in deceptive behavior, experts are permitted to do so if they rely on facts and data that are "of a type reasonably relied upon by experts in the particular field in forming opinions or inferences upon the subject" (Rule 703). All of the techniques and strategies reviewed in this volume have supporting research and are relied on in the practice of psychological assessment. More will be said about this in the next section on selection of test instruments.

A particularly interesting aspect of the *Daubert* decision that has direct relevance to forensic practitioners is the enumeration in Justice Blackmun's opinion of the criteria that courts may consider when determining if scientific evidence is admissible. These criteria are listed in Exhibit 5.1 and can be used to guide selection of various assessment techniques and to frame supportive arguments when defending one's procedures in court.

The first standard listed in Exhibit 5.1 calls for theories and techniques that form the basis of expert opinion to be empirically testable. As previous chapters have shown, ample research exists on the development of deception in children and adolescents. In addition, the techniques used to assess adolescents in clinical settings have been the focus

---

Exhibit 5.1

Daubert Standards for Admissibility of Scientific Evidence

- Empirically testable theory and/or techniques
- Peer review and publication
- Established rate of error
- General acceptance
- Reliability
- Validity
- Relevance

These criteria are not definitive or exhaustive and are meant only as a guide for courts to consider in deciding on the admissibility of scientific evidence. They can also inform clinicians who select particular instruments for use in forensic contexts.

of some attention. Although the research on adolescent malingering is scant, the theories discussed in chapter 2 and the techniques reviewed in chapters 3 and 4 are clearly capable of being, and in some cases have been, subjected to empirical testing. Also, literature on the SIRS, MMPI–A, MACI, and Rorschach cited in earlier chapters has been subjected to peer review and publication. Earlier chapters have provided support for the validity of these instruments. It is the focus of this discussion to provide a framework for making supportive arguments concerning the admissibility of testimony on adolescent malingering under the *Daubert* standards. Thus, it could be safely argued that the topic of adolescent malingering and the techniques used to assess response bias in adolescents is empirically testable and subject to peer review and publication. In the next section of this chapter on testifying about diagnostic power, I will offer more detail to demonstrate how other *Daubert* standards are satisfied with respect to adolescent assessment techniques, including their general acceptance, rate of error, reliability, and relevance.

Testifying About Diagnostic Efficiency

The *Daubert* opinion states that one major factor that should be taken into account when determining the admissibility of expert testimony is whether or not a rate of error has been established for the methods being offered. With respect to psychological assessment, the key concepts in determining accuracy of diagnostic decisions are found in operating characteristics of specific instruments (Baldessarini, Finkelstein, & Arana, 1983; Gibertini, Brandenburg, & Retzlaff, 1986). In particular, the operating characteristics of psychological instruments consist of the statistical properties of sensitivity, specificity, positive predictive power, negative predictive power, and overall diagnostic power. These statistics are represented in Table 5.1. To calculate operating characteristics, one must rely on some test score indicator of a diagnosis or condition. For example, the conclusion that an adolescent is malingering might be supported by an elevation on Scale *F* from the MMPI–A that exceeds a T-score of 80, or by three out of the eight SIRS scales falling in the Probable range. These examples are commonly referred to as test score

Table 5.1
Diagnostic Classification Statistics

Actual diagnosis	Diagnostic test indicator		Total
	Present	Absent	
Present	True positive (TP)	False negative (FN)	TP + FN
Absent	False positive (FP)	True negative (TN)	FP + TN
			N

NOTE: Population base rate or prevalence = (TP + FN)/N; sensitivity or true positive rate = TP/(TP + FN); specificity or true negative rate = TN/(FP + TN); positive predictive power (PPP) = TP/(TP + FP); negative predictive power (NPP) = TN/(FN + TN); overall diagnostic power = (TP + TN)/N.

cutoffs or indicators of malingering. A second factor that must be known in order to establish operating characteristics is the "actual diagnosis" of the individual. In cases of adolescent malingering, the status of the individual as a malingerer or bona fide patient is difficult to establish because of the difficulty in making an accurate diagnosis independently of test scores or other data. There is no ideal "gold standard" against which to evaluate an adolescent's propensity to dissimulate, and thus, research has generally relied on simulation studies in which participants are instructed to deliberately feign illness, experimentally producing an actual diagnosis against which to evaluate various test cutting scores.

The sensitivity of a test refers to the true positive rate, or the percentage of individuals who actually have the diagnosis or condition that is picked up by the test. In Table 5.1, test sensitivity is calculated by dividing the number of true positives by the total number of individuals who actually have the diagnosis. Specificity refers to the true negative rate, or the percentage of individuals who do not have the diagnosis who are accurately shown to not have the diagnosis on the test. To calculate specificity, one divides the number of true negatives by the number of individuals who do not have the disorder. Positive predictive power refers to the percentage of individuals testing positive on a test who actually have the diagnosis. This measure is obtained by dividing the true positive rate by the total number of individuals who have tested positive on the instrument. Negative predictive power is the percentage of individuals scoring negative on the test who do not have the diagnosis. This statistic is calculated by dividing the true negative rate by the total number of individuals who have scored negative on the test. Overall diagnostic power refers to the combined true positive and true negative rate, calculated by dividing the total number of true positives and true negatives by the total number of individuals in the population being evaluated.

As the foregoing descriptions illustrate, concepts involved in establishing diagnostic efficiency can be confusing and cumbersome, particularly when the expert attempts to convey this material to the trier of fact. Therefore, it is frequently helpful to put these concepts into practical terms that are much easier to grasp by reframing each of the statistics as a percentage that has meaning for the audience whom the expert is addressing (see Table 5.2). Because clinicians approach psychological evaluations from the standpoint of not knowing whether or not an adolescent belongs in a particular classification (e.g., psychotic, malingering), the task is to determine an appropriate diagnosis or assign a particular classification. Therefore, positive and negative predictive power are of greater use to practitioners than are sensitivity and specificity because practitioners typically start with test results or other data and attempt to assign a diagnosis (Meehl & Rosen, 1955). Positive and negative predictive power permit the practitioner to cite a level of confidence, or "rate of error," when drawing conclusions based on test scores alone. The clinician can then increase or decrease his or her level of confidence by adding data from clinical interviews, collateral resources, and other assessment data. The use of diagnostic efficiency statistics is one way of satisfying the rate of error standard outlined in the *Daubert* decision.

A major difficulty with most psychometric instruments used to detect malingering is that they do not cite diagnostic efficiency statistics for particular scales and cutoffs. There is a need for much more research in this area, not only for adolescents but for adult populations as well.

Table 5.2
Practical Interpretation of Diagnostic Efficiency Statistics

Statistic	Meaning of statistic
Base rate/prevalence	Percentage of the population that has the disorder/ condition
Sensitivity	Knowing the person has the condition/disorder; the likelihood the test will pick it up
Specificity	Knowing the person does not have the condition/ disorder; the likelihood the test will show it to not be present
Positive predictive power	Knowing the test is positive; the likelihood the person actually has the condition/disorder
Negative predictive power	Knowing the test is negative; the likelihood the person actually does not have the condition/disorder
Overall diagnostic power	Percentage of correct classifications by the test

Exceptions to this state of affairs are the SIRS and MMPI–A, which have some data on negative and positive predictive power values; these are cited in Tables 3.1, 3.2, and 4.2. An example that uses data from these tables will clarify how they can be of great use in actual practice.

Suppose while evaluating an adolescent, a clinician administers the MMPI–A and obtains an F-minus-K index of 9. Using values listed in Table 4.2, the clinician finds that this particular adolescent has scored below a cutoff of 10. Turning to the negative predictive power of 0.59, the clinician can be 59% confident that the adolescent is not malingering, based on the test indicator alone. This level of confidence is not overwhelming, considering that the base rate of malingering in the study that produced this negative predictive power was 50%; therefore, the F-minus-K index gives only a 9% increase over chance levels. The clinician can then turn to the T-score on Scale F and in this case the adolescent has obtained a T-score of 72. Since this falls below the T > 81 cutoff in Table 4.2, the negative predictive power shows that the clinician's confidence that the adolescent is not malingering jumps to 91%. This is fairly strong evidence that is further solidified by other test data. The MACI reveals a scale Z BR score of 69, placing the adolescent in roughly the 75th percentile (see Table 4.4), and the clinical interview reveals clear evidence of depression that is supported by collateral reports from the adolescent's parents.

In this example, the operating characteristics provide a baseline rate of error from which the expert can start the diagnostic decision-making process; supplemental data and information can then be used to confirm or disconfirm clinical hypotheses. The clinician used the MMPI–A scale F T-score to increase confidence from 59% to 91%. The MACI, interview, and collateral information were then used to confirm the opinion that the adolescent actually fell in the 91% range of "true negatives," that the adolescent was not malingering, and to rule out that the adolescent was in the 9% range of "false negatives" who are actually malingerers. The trick to using operating characteristics in this fashion is to explain their effective use to the trier of fact without confusing a judge or jury. Likewise, the expert should be careful not to fall into traps when using diagnostic efficiency statistics as the following comments will illustrate.

One potential source of error in using predictive power statistics is to operate under the assumption that these rates are constants and will not vary. Gibertini et al. (1986) have demonstrated how both positive and negative power are highly dependent on the prevalence of the disorder's being measured in the population being considered. The positive and negative predictive power values cited in chapters 3 and 4 are based on research studies in which the prevalence of malingering has been experimentally manipulated to be either 33% or 50%, percentages that are extremely high for many practical applications. Clearly, prevalence rates of malingering are likely to be much lower for many clinical settings and will vary across different settings such as in forensic evaluations. For instance, malingering would be expected to be more prevalent among the population of defendants raising an insanity defense than it would be for a general inpatient clinical population. Therefore, strict reliance on the diagnostic power rates from Table 4.2 in the previous example is technically an error, because it is unlikely that the base rate of malingering is 33% or 50% in clinical or forensic settings.

To address these concerns, Gibertini and his colleagues (1986) offered the following equations that can be used by clinicians:

$$PPP = \frac{Prevalence \times Sensitivity}{Prevalence \times Sensitivity + (1 - Prevalence) \times (1 - Specificity)}$$

$$NPP = \frac{Specificity \times (1 - Prevalence)}{Specificity \times (1 - Prevalence) + Prevalence \times (1 - Sensitivity)}$$

To use these equations, however, clinicians must know the sensitivity and specificity of the test being used, which are assumed to be constants, and the prevalence of the construct being assessed. The prevalence of definite or suspected malingering in clinical and forensic practice has been estimated to be about 13% to 15% (Rogers, Sewell, & Goldstein, 1994; Yates et al., 1996). Rogers, Hinds, and Sewell (1996) considered a base rate of 15% to be a good estimate of malingering in adolescent populations. My experiences suggest that the base rate of malingering is lower than 15% in clinical settings and is probably about 5% to 10%, whereas the base rate in forensic settings is around 15% to 20%. The base rate of other forms of deception, such as denial, is much greater in both clinical and forensic settings. Better estimates of positive and negative predictive power can be obtained by using sensitivity and specificity and an estimated prevalence rate of 15% from research studies.

Another problem plaguing use of diagnostic efficiency statistics is that some clinical decisions about adolescent dissimulation go beyond a simple "present or absent" level of analysis. Diagnostic efficiency statistics can be useful for providing a degree of confidence in one's decisions, but these statistics yield a percentage of certainty only for a particular individual test score. However, assessments involving the credibility of adolescent self-reports involve an array of possible response styles. The array of possible self-report styles includes denial, minimization, malingering, exaggeration of bona fide symptoms, social desirability, and even combinations of these response styles in a single case. Moreover, there are varying degrees of severity in each of these response styles. Therefore, diagnostic efficiency statistics are helpful, but they do not replace sound clinical judgment. Sometimes a unique or highly special case requires more than just direct reliance on efficiency statistics.

Finally, experts who rely on these statistics should not be misled into providing inaccurate statements by those who do not have a clear understanding of the significance of these statistics. Both attorneys who cross-examine the expert and lay individuals who observe such testimony may draw incorrect inferences from the data unless the clinician is clear about the meaning of these statistics. As explained by McCann and Dyer (1996), improper use of test operating characteristics can create misleading impressions. It is extremely important to examine the prevalence or base rate of the condition being measured against the predictive power of a test, because the base rate of a disorder represents the chance level that the particular disorder or condition is present. For example, a positive predictive power of 48% for a particular test may be wrongly interpreted as no better than the 50–50 chance that one would expect if a coin were flipped to make a decision. However, this argument completely ignores the base rate of malingering. Suppose that in the sample under consideration, the prevalence of malingering is only 15%. At chance levels, there is only a 15% chance that the adolescent would be classified correctly as malingering, but with the test, our confidence jumps to 48%. The test performs over three times better than chance alone, *not* merely as well as chance, as the erroneous argument would have one believe. It is then up to the clinician to collect all relevant information to determine whether the individual fits in the 48% who have the disorder or the 52% who do not. This integrative approach to data analysis helps to solidify one's ultimate conclusion.

These pitfalls and traps are extremely important to recognize when making use of diagnostic efficiency statistics in clinical and forensic settings. That is, "testifying about operating characteristics can be extremely persuasive if one is aware of the pitfalls and damaging to credibility if one does not recognize such traps" (McCann & Dyer, 1996, p. 164). Although some may question whether such detailed analysis of test operating characteristics in courtroom settings is ever necessary, my experience has shown that their use is of great interest to attorneys and judges alike, for they remove expert testimony from the realm of speculation and conjecture and place it more firmly in a scientific and technical framework within which all experts strive to work.

SELECTING TESTS AND INSTRUMENTS IN FORENSIC EVALUATIONS

Recall that another consideration under a *Daubert* test of the admissibility of expert testimony is general acceptance of the scientific methology. Although rules of evidence have the most influence over whether or not expert testimony will be admissible, clinicians can also look to standards within the profession as a guide for selecting the most appropriate assessment techniques and methods. In fact, professional standards are very useful in supporting the foundations of one's testimony because they can serve to establish the general acceptance of one's methods in forensic evaluations.

Heilbrun (1992) has outlined seven criteria that can serve as a guideline for selecting test instruments in forensic settings. The first criterion, according to Heilbrun, is that the test be commercially available. Moreover, it is recommended that a test be accompanied by a technical manual that describes development of the instrument, specific psychometric properties, and administration procedures. Also recommended is that the test be subjected to some form of peer review such as a *Mental Measurements Yearbook* or scientific journal review. The existence of a manual permits documentation of proper administration procedures and psychometric properties that can be raised on cross-examination and rebuttal evidence.

A second major criterion suggested by Heilbrun is that the instrument be psychometrically reliable. It is important to note that reliability here refers to psychometric reliability, or the precision (i.e., internal consistency) and stability (i.e., test–retest) of a psychological test instrument. Lawyers typically use the term *reliable* in a manner that denotes validity, or whether or not the test measures what it purports to measure (McCann & Dyer, 1996). With respect to psychometric reliability, Heilbrun made the recommendation that a reliability coefficient of less than 0.80 not be considered advisable unless the expert can provide "explicit justification" for why the test was used. Toward this end, both internal consistency and test–retest reliability are relevant, although McCann and Dyer (1996) provided a discussion as to why internal consistency, or precision of a one-time administration, is more important for determining the reliability of a psychological test instrument.

The third criterion suggested by Heilbrun is that the test have some direct relevance to the legal issue being examined. Moreover, it is strongly recommended that this relevance be documented by availability of specific validation research that is published in peer-reviewed journals. The relevance of psychological test instruments to the issue of adolescent malingering and deception is of particular importance, since many of the instruments reviewed in chapters 3 and 4 are suitable for measuring adolescent response styles. It should be noted, however, that rarely is the sole referral question in forensic evaluations the determination of malingering. Rather, malingering typically is a collateral or secondary issue to a more significant psycholegal question such as competency to stand trial, treatability, or criminal responsibility.

A fourth criterion recommended by Heilbrun is that there be some standard administration format that is used when administering a psychological test. Most objective instruments, such as the SIRS, MMPI–A, or MACI, have standard administration instructions printed on the test booklet. One instrument that raises concerns in this regard is the Rorschach, due to the history of various administration and scoring procedures. When the Rorschach is being used to provide relevant data regarding the veracity of an adolescent's self-reported psychopathology, the Exner Comprehensive System (Exner, 1991, 1993; Exner & Weiner, 1982) is recommended for a standardized administration and scoring procedure, because much of the current research on the Rorschach is based on this system.

The fifth criterion noted by Heilbrun is applicability of the test to the population that is being examined. With respect to forensic assessment of adolescents, it is very important that instruments designed specifically for adolescents or which have well-developed normative data on adolescent populations be available. As noted in earlier chapters, most of the instruments that are useful in assessing adolescent dissimulation have been designed for adolescents (e.g., MMPI–A, MACI) or have established normative data on adolescents (e.g., Rorschach).

The sixth criterion outlined by Heilbrun is that objective tests with actuarial data are preferable to those that do not permit actuarially based interpretation. There have been specific attempts to work toward actuarial data for the assessment of malingering in adolescents, using the MMPI–A and SIRS, both of which are objective assessment instruments. Moreover, many of the instruments reviewed are well suited for the development of actuarial data because they permit cutoff scores and diagnostic algorithms to be established. However, much research is needed to reach this ideal state of affairs.

Finally, Heilbrun lists as a seventh criterion for selecting psychological tests in forensic settings that evaluation of response style or biased responding be possible with the instrument being used. Toward this end, the reviews in chapters 3 and 4 attempt to provide some research base for establishing the utility of major psychological assessment instruments in forensic evaluation of adolescents. Interestingly, Heilbrun (1992) made the statement that the "only psychological test with extensive empirical support in measuring response style is the MMPI" (p. 268). Although this statement is not true for the adult version of the MMPI,[1] it can be stated with some degree of accuracy that the MMPI–A and SIRS are the only two instruments whose utility in assessing adolescent malingering has been the object of any significant degree of research. The MACI, although having scales that are relevant to self-report biases, has not been the focus of extensive research. This is particularly unfortunate because the MACI holds several distinct advantages over the MMPI–A in assessing adolescent psycho-

---

[1]The MCMI–II (McCann & Dyer, 1996) and Personality Assessment Instrument (Morey, 1996) are examples of two other adult instruments with a body of research documenting their utility in assessing malingering and dissimulation in adults.

pathology. These advantages include the brevity of the MACI (160 items) compared with the MMPI–A (478 items), the broader age range of the MACI (13 to 19) as opposed to that of the MMPI–A (14 to 18), the lower reading level required for the MACI (sixth grade; Millon, 1993) compared with that for the MMPI–A (seventh grade; Archer, 1992), and the MACI's superior internal-consistency and sensitivity to base rate considerations in calibrating scores. Clinical experiences have also shown the MACI to provide much more useful clinical information than does MMPI–A. Therefore, a very fruitful area of research would be the development of adequate cutoffs on the MACI for evaluating dissimulation.

Overall, there is scant research on any one instrument as an accurate measure of adolescent malingering and dissimulation. Therefore, a particular instrument may have relevance to a specific issue in an adolescent forensic examination, but the use of any one instrument should be directed at corroborating clinical hypotheses rather than making definitive diagnostic conclusions.

The criteria outlined by Heilbrun serve as a useful guideline, but they are not a set of absolute criteria; this is particularly so for adolescent assessment instruments because the research base is extremely limited. No single assessment instrument meets each and every criterion suggested by Heilbrun. For example, the MMPI–A has some research supporting its use in the assessment of malingering, but it fails to meet the criterion of a reliability coefficient of 0.80 or higher. As noted in the MMPI–A manual (Butcher et al., 1992) only 3 out of the 13 validity and clinical scales on the instrument meet or exceed the 0.80 criterion with respect to internal consistency for a clinical sample of boys (see Butcher et al., 1992, Table 14, p. 52), and only 5 of the scales exceed this criterion for a clinical sample of girls (see Butcher et al., 1992, Table 14, p. 52). Only 5 of the 13 validity and clinical MMPI–A scales exceed the 0.80 criterion for test–retest reliability (Butcher et al., 1992, Table 13, p. 51). The MACI scales, on the other hand, have much better reliability, but there have been no empirically derived cutoffs for establishing the likelihood of malingering. Therefore, while Heilbrun's criteria serve as a guideline for selecting the most relevant and accurate instruments for assessing adolescents in forensic settings, the major instruments currently available may meet many, but not necessarily all, of these criteria. Exhibit 5.2 summarizes these criteria for reference when selecting instruments in adolescent forensic assessments.

A second format for selecting psychometric instruments in forensic settings has been set forth by Marlowe (1995), which has been termed a *hybrid decision framework*. According to this model, a set of decisions can be made to operationalize criteria for selecting specific instruments. Interestingly, the criteria in Marlowe's model are similar to those outlined by Heilbrun (1992). The initial step in selecting psychometric instruments for use in forensic settings is to determine if the role of the expert satisfies a requirement that the scientific and technical knowledge be truly specialized. Second, the theory or underlying body of knowledge should be time tested and there should be a sufficient body of literature to support use of the instrument. The third step in Marlowe's framework is to determine whether or not the instrument on which an expert relies has items that sample all relevant content domains and provides an adequate range of items. Moreover, there should

---

Exhibit 5.2

Heilbrun's (1992) Guidelines for Test Selection in Forensic Evaluations

- Commercial Availability—accompanied by technical manual and peer reviewed.
- Reliability—recommend .80 or higher or explicit justification.
- Relevant Test—relevance to legal issue and appropriate validation research.
- Standard Administration Procedures
- Applicability to population being tested.
- Actuarial Data—objective tests preferred.
- Response Style Evaluation—some method for determining validity of test results.

be a standard method for administration and appropriate group norms; in short, the test should have adequate psychometric properties of content validity and reliability. Fourth in the framework is the question of whether or not data collected and analyzed through administration of the test are sound; at this step, the professional must be capable of making a determination as to the integrity of the data for the specific case under consideration. In particular, such an analysis looks at such issues as whether or not standard administration procedures were followed, justified norms were applied to the individual being examined, and statistical manipulation of the data followed generally accepted procedures. An example of this process would be calculation of WISC–III deviation IQ scores for the three factors of verbal comprehension, perceptual–organizational, and freedom from distractibility.

The final set of issues that Marlowe outlined as part of his hybrid framework has to do with whether or not data derived from particular psychological tests are irrelevant, duplicative, or prejudicial. Also, issues concerning the appropriate expert reasoning that was used in arriving at conclusions from the test data are also an important consideration in evaluating psychometric data. In particular, one of the specific issues that courts are directed to look at is the specific psycholegal formulation that the expert made and the manner in which criteria were operationalized. Moreover, the expert must make sure that there are empirical foundations from which conclusions may be drawn, and the expert must provide a reasonable level of certainty about those conclusions.

To help organize test data and diagnostic conclusions according to Marlowe's hybrid model, Exhibit 5.3 presents the major criteria for this model. Essentially, the hybrid model suggests that forensic practitioners evaluate their procedures, data analysis, conclusions, and reasoning at every step of the examination to make sure that they are legally defensible when offered as evidence in a legal proceeding.

The proposals offered by Marlowe (1995) and Heilbrun (1992) contain common themes that can be considered when selecting instruments for the issue of malingering and dissimulation in adolescent populations. In particular, psychological test instruments should be well recognized and generally accepted within the field. Several methods exist

---

Exhibit 5.3

Marlowe's (1995) Hybrid Framework for Evaluating Psychometric Evidence

- Recognition of the expert witness: unique access; data not easily accessible
- Recognition of the underlying theory: time tested; falsifiable; commitment to refinement
- Recognition of the instrument or test: content domain; reliability; standardization; adherence to professional standards
- Appropriate data collection, reduction, and analysis: standardized administration; justified norms; justified data reduction and analysis
- Data not irrelevant, prejudicial, or duplicative
- No countervailing social policies against test use
- Valid expert reasoning linking data to conclusions: psycholegal formation; explicit empirical bases; data modifiers; fulcrum of debate; express level of certainty

---

for determining acceptance, such as commercial availability, the publication of a technical manual, peer review, and publication of research in professional journals. With the exception of Statement Reality Analysis, which does not have a standardized scoring and administration method currently established, despite the existence of research supporting its utility, and clinical interview methods, which represent generally accepted procedures that do not really constitute a formal psychological test, the instruments and procedures reviewed in chapters 3 and 4 meet this criterion. A second common theme in Marlowe's and Heilbrun's formulations is that psychological tests should have an adequate level of reliability and research supporting their validity. Other themes emerging from these two models include the fact that psychological constructs being measured by psychological tests should have direct relevance to the legal issues being evaluated, adequate norms should be available, and data must not be analyzed or interpreted in novel or idiosyncratic ways.

Although none of the psychological instruments discussed in earlier chapters satisfy each and every criterion of these two models, all have relevance to many of the issues commonly examined in adolescent forensic examination. For example, the Rorschach is commercially available, has highly standardized methods for administration, has adequate test–retest reliability (Exner, 1993), and research supporting the use of some ratios and indices for identifying potential malingering; however, there are no well-developed actuarial data on the Rorschach indices of malingering and dissimulation currently available. Thus, each major psychological test instrument has particular strengths and weaknesses, and definitive diagnostic conclusions cannot be drawn from any single test or scale. Each of the instruments satisfies many criteria, but they should be used in a cumulative fashion to corroborate hypotheses and to assist in rendering conclusions.

CONCLUSION

The practice of diagnosing psychopathology in adolescence is a challenging task. When diagnostic issues become concerned with the likelihood of malingering and deception, the challenge increases because of the potential adverse impact on the individual teenager. Determination of whether or not an adolescent is malingering can have profound effects on treatment plans, clinical staff perceptions of the teenager, or the legal disposition or management of a case. Therefore, the practitioner should maintain an awareness of the ethical and professional issues involved, including adherence to professional standards and making sure that findings and conclusions are not misused.

In many cases, the mental health professional may also be called on to provide testimony in court matters. It is therefore important to have some awareness of the legal tests and standards that are used to evaluate the admissibility of various forms of expert testimony. The major legal standards include the FRE, the *Frye* test, and the recent *Daubert* standard. Using these legal tests, as well as guidelines recently outlined in the scientific and professional literature, parameters are set forth for selecting appropriate assessment techniques and presenting opinions and testimony in a coherent manner.

Although there is no perfect method—be it clinical interview or psychological test—for assessing malingering, each of the techniques discussed in earlier chapters has a number of strengths. Within the context of a clinical and forensic assessment, a comprehensive, multi-method evaluation provides the most ethical, responsible, and legally defensible approach.

6

Applications in Clinical Settings

The nature of the setting in which one practices has a direct impact on the assessment process according to a number of factors. Base rates for particular disorders can vary across settings; the context in which an evaluation is conducted can affect the data on which opinions are based; and treatment interventions vary, depending on their suitability or effectiveness. There are pronounced differences between the role of mental health professional as clinician-therapist and forensic evaluator-consultant. As discussed in chapter 1, clinicians and forensic professionals differ with respect to the clients they ultimately serve, the degree of advocacy they offer for the patient-litigant, the assumptions made about the trustworthiness of the individual, and the strategies and techniques used to accomplish their goals. It has been emphasized that the blending of clinical and forensic roles should be avoided (Greenberg & Shuman, 1997; Kuehnle, 1996).

In the case of adolescents who are seen in clinical settings, the ability to assess accuracy of self-reports and to identify attempts at feigning symptoms is a necessary part of any evaluation to ensure that the adolescent receives appropriate treatment. Empirical research can provide useful information for the clinician, but the challenge is to

make practical use of the research findings. On the other hand, anec-
dotal case material illustrates practical applications, but the approaches
used in one case may not generalize to other cases. Throughout previous chapters, there was very little case material used to illustrate practical strategies for making assessments of the veracity of adolescent self-
reports. The major reason for excluding significant case material until
now is because the multimethod approach to evaluating dissimulation
in adolescents requires that basic material be presented first. In this
way, case examples can build on the information contained in earlier
chapters.

In this chapter and the one that follows, I will present several
clinical and forensic cases in which the veracity and accuracy of
adolescent self-reports are key issues. By way of introduction, this
chapter addresses denial, symptom exaggeration, and symptom
coaching in clinical settings to provide some direction for clinical
practice. After an introductory discussion of general treatment issues, I will discuss the role of various defense processes in the presentation of clinical syndromes and will review the issues involved
in formulating effective treatment strategies. Specific cases will be
used to explore how denial and minimization create difficulties in
treatment and how symptom overreporting and exaggeration in
clinical settings are often manifestations of more severe forms of
psychopathology.

Although cases of pure malingering are found in clinical settings,
the more prototypic case of interest to those working in a therapeutic,
as opposed to forensic, capacity is the adolescent who exaggerates or
overreports symptoms as part of a more pervasive form of psychopathology (e.g., borderline personality disorder, dissociative disorder) or
who does so within the context of an intractable situational problem
(e.g., severe family conflict, shared familial psychosis). In other instances, parental attempts at symptom coaching can be reflective of a
disrupted family system that becomes the focus of treatment; a clinical
illustration will be used to explore these issues. The case examples for
this chapter were selected based on their ability to illustrate relevant
treatment issues.

GENERAL TREATMENT ISSUES

Treatment in the mental health professions assumes a working alliance between the patient who enters psychotherapy to relieve symptoms or improve functioning and a professional who has experience and skill in alleviating problematic symptoms. In fact, a good working alliance can be viewed as perhaps one of the most important factors that predicts positive outcome in psychotherapy. When the patient fails to provide honest, reliable, or accurate information to the therapist, it follows that the working alliance is threatened. Malingering and other forms of deception, such as denial or symptom exaggeration, are threats to a working alliance because they interfere with honest communication between patient and therapist.

All too often, an underlying assumption that exists in many clinical settings is that malingering is a diagnosis that dooms patients to be labeled as "fakers" or "manipulators" who are then cast aside and labeled as untreatable. Although these perceptions may be accurate in a few cases, these biases should be eliminated for the most part from clinical practice. That is, a patient, particularly an adolescent, who is exaggerating his or her symptomatology should not necessarily be viewed as a patient unworthy of treatment. At various points throughout earlier chapters, it was suggested that one of the key questions to be answered once an adolescent has been deemed to be dissimulating is, What are the contextual factors, or underlying motivations for the adolescent presenting as he or she does? Oftentimes, very important clinical information can be obtained by exploring contextual and motivational factors that maintain deceptive presentations. For example, an adolescent may feign somatic complaints to avoid school, where the teenager faces anxiety-provoking peer interactions or some other social pressure. Perhaps the adolescent feigns psychosis or suicidal ideation to escape a chaotic or abusive family situation. If an adolescent malingerer is quickly dismissed as a manipulator, valuable opportunities for productive and helpful therapeutic intervention will be lost. Therefore, failure to consider underlying motivational and contextual factors that foster dissimulation, once it has been identified, should be considered an error in clinical practice.

157

Another valuable therapeutic guideline is to maintain a distinction between short-term and long-term treatment goals. It is not always desirable, or even possible, to expect an adolescent who denies or minimizes a problem to become less defensive and more open in a brief period of time. Likewise, an adolescent who feigns or exaggerates symptomatology will not generally abandon deceptive response patterns unless the factors providing the motivation to do so are no longer present. Thus, short-term goals should be both reasonable and attainable when they address response style issues. For example, the initial treatment goal with respect to adolescents who are resistant or denying problems may be to get them verbally invested in a discussion with the therapist about any general topic, not necessarily one that pertains to actual clinical problems. Also, one of the more immediate goals for adolescents believed to be malingering may be to engage in discussion that focuses away from symptoms of the feigned illness.

Because of threats to treatment posed by deceptive processes, a number of other principles should also be kept in mind. These issues can prove extremely useful in cases involving long-term therapy. My clinical observations reveal that most adolescents will exhibit some form of deceptive behavior, such as denial, resistance to treatment, symptom exaggeration, or other dissimulation. Therefore, therapists and ancillary treatment staff require high levels of empathy and patience when working with this population. It is relatively easy to become angered or frustrated with the lack of veracity that can occur in treatment among adolescent populations, and adverse reactions on the part of therapists and staff should be avoided. Ongoing peer supervision and regular staff meetings are methods for maintaining higher levels of empathy and patience among staff. In addition, one must be able to look beyond the adolescent's "label" or "diagnosis" to examine the contextual and motivational factors that are contributing to the dissimulation. Again, supervision from a peer or colleague can be extremely valuable. Treatment teams in hospital or residential settings often have intense contact with adolescents on a daily basis, and some patients can produce countertransference reactions in large segments of the team; sometimes entire treatment teams may lose their capacity to empathize or effectively treat particularly challenging adolescents. In these instances, the use of a neutral third party who is outside the normal staffing patterns can maintain a check on these impediments to treatment.

DEFENSIVENESS AND DENIAL IN ADOLESCENT TREATMENT

Perhaps one of the most challenging aspects of working with adolescent populations in clinical practice is effectively dealing with denial and other forms of resistance. It is indeed rare to find an adolescent who willingly or compliantly enters into therapy. Treatment of adolescents in psychotherapy necessarily involves developing a working alliance with the adolescent and breaking through the resistance in order to bring about improvement or change; therefore, denial and resistance are often much more challenging in clinical settings.

Many useful approaches to overcoming resistance in therapy with adolescents have been summarized nicely by Wexler (1991). The framework outlined by Wexler operates under the assumption that adolescents who exhibit psychological and behavioral disturbances do so because they have attempted to cope with difficult and trying circumstances with very limited psychological resources. As a result, adolescent disturbances are viewed as deficits in self-regulation, self-control, self-esteem, and self-efficacy. Using a theoretical model adapted from psychoanalytic self psychology, Wexler integrated cognitive–behavioral techniques to improve the self-regulatory capacities of adolescents.

In all, there are six major ways of addressing adolescent resistance outlined by Wexler that are placed under the general rubric of *reframing*. Accordingly, the effective dissolution of resistance in treatment involves avoiding power struggles and modifying mental constructs so that the adolescent can adopt more flexible and adaptive methods for coping. Therefore, Wexler favored a straightforward and consistent approach to interpreting and confronting adolescent resistance that may take the form of denial.

The first technique involves reinterpreting an adolescent's resistance or defensiveness as "making sense," in that it is a form of self-protective behavior. Many times, adolescents present for treatment and say very little, or when they do engage in conversation, they will often deny that there are any significant difficulties that they experience. Such defensive postures can frequently be understood as sensible in that they protect the adolescent from external stressors or threats. In this way, the re-framing of denial or defensiveness as understandable behaviors can decrease the likelihood that an adolescent will view the therapist's questions and comments as threatening and increases the chances of developing rapport and understanding that are so crucial to a good working alliance.

A second technique advocated by Wexler is providing adolescents with a greater sense of personal choice about the goals of treatment and the proposed changes they strive to make. Oftentimes, the goals of treatment are those that the parent or some other adult has selected. Although adolescents may half-heartedly agree with these goals, less resistance and greater cooperation are generated when the adolescent is challenged to select those goals that are important to him or her. For example, the teenager may state, "I guess my parents would get off my back if I just stopped hanging around with my current friends." This statement suggests that the adolescent is responding to what his parents think is important. Instead, personal choice is fostered by confronting the passivity: "But what do you feel is the most important change that you want to make?" Additionally, Wexler suggested that when adolescents withdraw from treatment and refuse to participate after some productive work, then a therapeutic stance of giving the teenager permission to "take care" of himself or herself when pressure mounts is an appropriate technique. Permitting some low levels of resistance and giving the adolescent permission to choose a course of conduct can serve therapeutic goals by limiting combative attacks on an adolescent's resistance.

Conflict seems to characterize most aspects of adolescence, as evidenced, for example, by the striving for independence and autonomy in the face of one's emotional and financial dependence on parents. Because of the turmoil surrounding this period of development, it comes as no surprise that "adolescents are obsessed with power" (Wexler, 1991, p. 98). Resistance and denial in psychotherapy represent the struggle for power and control in the treatment setting. What reframing permits is the therapist to redefine an adolescent's resistant, oppositional, and belligerent behavior as a *loss* of control. That is, the resistant behavior is viewed as a reaction to the demands or intrusions of parents or other authority figures and therefore directly "controlled" by persons other than the adolescent. Thus, an appropriate therapeutic response is to direct the adolescent to see that by relinquishing obstructive or resistant behavior, there is now a choice as to how one can react to any one situation. On the other hand, resistance leads to rigidity, which in turn limits freedom of choice in one's behavior, which is framed as a loss of control or power for the adolescent. This reframing technique is a third method for dealing therapeutically with resistant behavior.

A fourth strategy that Wexler offered for dealing with resistance in treatment is to reframe conflict-laden problems as an "opportunity." That is, some problems such as conflict with parents, rejection by peers, or even recent placement in a residential setting may generate intense negativity and resistance in adolescence. A therapeutic stance that views such situations as an opportunity to learn new forms of behavior and techniques for resolving conflict can often help to break through strong denial or resistance.

Another technique for addressing resistance and denial in treatment is to carefully examine an adolescent's expectations about the possible outcome of a problem situation. Adolescents will typically deny problems or difficulties in the initial phase of treatment because they may have unrealistic expectations about the treatment setting. For instance, there may be concerns that problems will be reported back to parents, a probation officer, or some other authority figure. Moreover, the therapist may be viewed as another adult who is incapable of understanding teenage concerns. By addressing preconceived notions about the treatment setting, before dealing with specific problems, denial and resistance can sometimes be effectively resolved.

A final method for dealing with denial in adolescent treatment is "paradoxical intervention." The theory behind this strategy is that it is sometimes better to encourage or support some resistant behavior than engage in battles with the adolescent by actively attacking or challenging the resistance. For example, one form of paradoxical intervention is to prescribe obstructive behavior. In one case, a particularly difficult adolescent was being treated in a hospital setting, yet she was denying any knowledge of why her parents had her admitted; repeated attempts to explore issues met with failure. The teenager was then instructed to repeat these denials in a family meeting with the parents present and to make her case for discharge even more firmly in the family meeting. The result was a confrontation between the teenager and her parents in which very concrete evidence was produced of severely strained familial relationships. These data were then used to confront the teenager and contradict her claims that all was fine at home. Paradoxical interventions can be useful, but they also must be used cautiously; sometimes encouraging resistance only makes conflict more deeply entrenched. Some adolescents fail to respond and can challenge the "reverse psychology" stance of paradoxical techniques. Effective application of these strategies depends on proper timing and an appearance of sincerity on the part of the therapist.

There are various forms of resistance and denial in adolescent clinical settings. Some resistance is driven largely by situational factors such as placement in a residential setting or a recent hospitalization. In these and similar instances, denial is an adaptational response that is an effort to convince others that matters are fine so that the teenager can be released or discharged. In other instances, denial may be more pervasive and driven by characterological factors, such as narcissistic needs to appear healthy and well adjusted or to gain the approval of same-age peers. One of the most important steps to addressing defensiveness in treatment is to assess the underlying factors that maintain a resistant stance on the part of the adolescent. These factors may be situational, characterological, motivational, or contextual, and a number of hypotheses must be explored. The following case example illustrates how a number of the assessment strategies discussed in earlier chapters can be used to formulate an appropriate treatment plan that incorporates some of these treatment approaches.

Case Example: Barry

Barry is a 16-year-old White youth who was referred for a psychological evaluation after he assaulted another youth. He had been playing baseball with some friends, and they were teasing one another. After another youth began making disparaging remarks about Barry and his girlfriend, the confrontations escalated to the point that Barry seriously injured the other youth in a physical attack. The major issue to be addressed in the evaluation was the potential for Barry to benefit from treatment. Concerns were raised by his guidance counselor at school about the potential for Barry to be a "habitual criminal" who would never benefit from intervention. He was seen as superficial, denied the severity of his behavior, lacked empathy, and was seen as a poor candidate for rehabilitative services. His guidance counselor requested an evaluation to see if an appropriate treatment plan could be formulated.

The history revealed that Barry came from a family with numerous conflicts and difficulties. He had been adopted at an early age, so no information was available about his biological parents. His adoptive father was severely alcoholic, and the parents divorced when he was 5 years of age. He was described as extremely strong-willed throughout his childhood, and he repeatedly attempted to "take control of the household." On one occasion, he became physically assaultive toward his older sister, who was also adopted, although from a different set of biological parents. At school he was seen as bright and a very fast learner, but he was always aggressive and dominant with other children. In the many years since his parents' divorce, he had moved back and forth between his mother's and father's homes due to his behavioral difficulties. There were no prior arrests and no history of severe conduct problems such as fire setting, cruelty to animals, or use of weapons. Moreover, there was no history of substance abuse.

Interpersonally, Barry presented as a narcissistic adolescent who was extremely self-assured. He would frequently point out his talents and abilities and talked excessively about how "popular" he was at school and with girls in particular. On the mental status examination, he presented as a nice-looking youth who exhibited no disturbances in the form of his thinking or in the display of his emotions. Moreover, he denied the need for any treatment, as he felt that he was perfectly capable of handling his own affairs.

The psychological testing data presented in Exhibit 6.1 were obtained during a comprehensive evaluation. One major characteristic of the test results is that Barry is extremely defensive in the way that he presents his problems. There is no indication of random or inconsistent responding (MACI scale $VV = 0$; MMPI $VRIN = 45$). The MACI Desirability scale (Y) is elevated, and the MMPI–A validity scale configuration reveals a socially desirable response set, with scales L and K moderately elevated and scale F relatively low. Additional support for Barry's defensiveness is seen in his Rorschach record, with a somewhat abbreviated record ($R = 16$), the predominance of form as a determinant (*Lambda* $= 1.29$), and the presence of intellectualization as a defensive process ($2AB + Art + Ay = 5$). Overall, Barry approached the testing in a guarded fashion, attempting to portray himself in a positive light.

Despite his defensiveness, Barry projects an unrealistically positive image as a result of strong narcissistic personality characteristics. He presents as a grandiose, overly self-assured youth on interview, and this is supported by his elevation on the Egotistic *(5)* scale on the MACI (BR $= 83$). Moreover, despite his seeming lack of sensitivity to others and the pattern of conduct disturbance he has displayed, the testing indicates that he is capable of maintaining some interest in relationships with others (MACI scale $4 = 103$; Rorschach $T = 1$ and $H = 2$). However, his interpersonal relationships are characterized by his superficiality and sensitivity to narcissistic injury. Moreover, others are likely to be seen in terms of what they can do for him rather than as equals in a mutual "give-and-take" relationship.

In this particular case, Barry's defensiveness was not merely situational, although he was experiencing some situational tension due to legal difficulties he was facing as a result of the assault ($CDI =$ positive; $D = -2$ and $Adj.D = -1$). However, he also has strong characterological tendencies that make him extremely sensitive to negative appraisal and criticism. It is because of his narcissistic personality that his defensiveness is more deeply entrenched and is a more pervasive impediment to treatment.

Exhibit 6.1

Selected Psychological Test Results From Barry's Evaluation

I. MACI

VV	Reliability Index	0
X	Disclosure	30
Y	Desirability	78
Z	Debasement	35
4	Dramatizing	103
5	Egotistic	83

II. MMPI–A

VRIN	45
TRIN	62
F	42
L	63
K	63
F-minus-K	−17

III. Rorschach

$R = 16$

$EB = 1:1.0$

$FC:CF + C = 0:2$

$X + \% = .50$

$2AB + Art + Ay = 5$

$Lambda = 1.29$

$eb = 2:7$

$T = 1$

$F + \% = .56$

Constellations $= DEPI, CDI$

$D = -2 \quad Adj.D = -1$

$H = 2 \quad AG = 0$

$WSUM6 = 23$

Barry was seen as an appropriate candidate for intensive individual psychotherapy. With respect to potential "criminal tendencies" suggested by the guidance counselor, the conclusion was offered instead that Barry does not have strong psychopathic or antisocial personality traits; however, some antisocial acting out tends to be associated with his continuing efforts to prove his superiority to others, and the acting out may continue sporadically. He is more appropriately characterized by a narcissistic personality style, with a fragile sense of self and poor judgment leading him to act out at times. It was recommended that he enter into long-term individual psychotherapy from a self psychology perspective partly as a result of some positive prognostic signs (i.e., the capacity to form friendships, social interests, etc.) and the lack of any prior psychological treatment in the past. A self psychological therapeutic approach was recommended to increase the chances that Barry would respond positively to attempts at understanding him through empathic attunement rather than through a confrontational or cognitive–behavioral approach, in which interventions would be viewed by Barry as attacks on his fragile sense of self.

SYMPTOM OVERREPORTING IN TREATMENT SETTINGS

The "stress and storm" theory of adolescence has had a major impact on the way this period of development has been conceptualized (Archer & Ball, 1988; Grotevant, 1980). This approach to understanding symptoms of psychopathology is based on the observation that unusual, mildly pathological behavior and adjustment reactions are common in adolescents because of the emotional turmoil and environmental pressures that arise during the teenage years. In fact, Anna Freud (1958) suggested that most adolescents are expected to experience some form of emotional distress or behavioral acting out and that those adolescents who do not are at greater risk for more serious psychopathology as adults.

Various factors contribute to the emotional turmoil of adolescence. Among these are biological pressures brought on by rapid physical maturation and hormonal changes. There are also social pressures such as peer group influences and psychological conflicts surrounding identity formulation and conflict with parents over growing autonomy needs. Because of the greater levels of stress during adolescence, it is not surprising that research has shown adolescents to report higher levels of unusual symptoms and problems (Archer & Ball, 1988).

Despite the expectation of higher levels of emotional turmoil and distress in adolescence, the overreporting of symptoms is not the product of malingering in the absence of some clear material secondary gain. Instead, elevated levels of self-reported pathology typically represent genuine psychopathology. More specifically, adolescents may present with many different complaints, such as anxiety, depressive symptoms, vague thought processes, identity confusion, and a litany of family problems. These symptoms may at times be viewed as an indiscriminate endorsement of symptoms that often accompanies malingering or other forms of intentional dissimulation. However, not all such symptom presentations necessarily reflect malingering, particularly if they arise in clinical treatment settings, as opposed to forensic settings, or when there are identifiable and confirmable environmental stressors.

The presence of numerous symptoms can result from the breakdown of already weakened coping mechanisms. Adolescents with intellectual deficits, borderline personality disturbances, chaotic family situations, impulse control difficulties, and substance abuse propensities typically are poor problem-solvers, and they experience high levels of tension and stress. Moreover, they have deficits in their coping ability that render them ill-equipped to manage the problems they encounter when under stress. Thus, the resultant symptoms may be manifestations of weakened reality testing, identity confusion, or unsophisticated pleas for help from others, rather than malingering.

The differentiation between malingering or intentional dissimulation and symptom overreporting that is a product of severe psychopathology can sometimes be facilitated by examining the context of the evaluation. Factors that increase the likelihood of genuine psychopathology include (a) a clinical as opposed to forensic setting, (b) identifiable environmental stressors that would create distress in most adolescents (e.g., physical abuse), (c) clinical presentation that is consistent with severe psychopathology, (d) intellectual deficits, (e) prior psychiatric history, and (f) secondary gain that has psychological (e.g., attention from an ex-boyfriend or ex-girlfriend, removal from an abusive household) as opposed to material (e.g., release from custody, time off from school) significance. Although the list of potential factors may be considerable, the factors listed here represent those that have proven to be clinically useful in distinguishing between malingering and overreporting as a symptom of genuine psychopathology.

The following case illustrates how a wide range of emotional and behavioral difficulties were reported by an adolescent in response to several stressors. These reports revealed high levels of psychopathology that were evident from psychological testing. Rather than as reflecting attempts to manipulate the situation, the overreporting was seen as the product of a teenager with a borderline personality organization who was encountering severe threats to his emotional security.

Case Example: Robert

Robert is a 15-year-old White youth who was admitted to an adolescent inpatient psychiatric unit. The admission was precipitated when he threatened to kill his parents and then ran away from home. He had just recently been discharged from another hospital where he had been admitted due to escalating conduct problems. These problems included threatening a teacher and stalking his ex-girlfriend after she ended their relationship several weeks earlier because of his extremely jealous and controlling behavior.

His history revealed that he was born into a very abusive and chaotic family in which his father had schizophrenia and his mother was extremely neglectful. After being subjected to horrendous physical abuse as an infant and toddler, such as being burned with cigarettes and placed in scalding baths, he was placed in foster care at the age of 5. After numerous placements, the parental rights of his biological parents were terminated and Robert was adopted at the age of 8 by a family with one older child. His adjustment was poor overall; he had problems with authority, and his adoptive parents had difficulty controlling him.

At the time of his recent admission, he exhibited irritable and depressive affect, and his thinking was paranoid and suspicious but not delusional. He experienced intermittent homicidal ideation toward his adoptive parents, whom he saw as responsible for alienating his ex-girlfriend. In fact, the parents were attempting to keep Robert away from her for his own protection, because the ex-girlfriend had obtained an order of protection to shield herself from Robert's aggressive stalking behavior. He had violated an order in the past by breaking into her home, and he was at risk for more serious charges. Robert's intellectual functioning was in the average range, and there was no evidence of attentional problems or memory difficulties according to previous intellectual and neuropsychological testing.

Selected results from the psychological testing conducted with Robert upon his admission are presented in Exhibit 6.2. A major characteristic of the self-report data on the MACI and MMPI–A is that Robert has adopted a response set that points to overreporting of problems. The MACI shows an extremely high elevation on Debasement (scale Z) at a BR of 100, suggesting that Robert is focusing on the negative aspects of himself and his current situation. Moreover, the MMPI–A elevation on scale F (T = 65) is rather high, and his F-minus-K index is also elevated, although less than the most efficient cutoff for identifying malingering (see Table 4.2). Despite the significance of these elevations on scales representing symptom overreporting, a perusal of the remaining test results in Exhibit 6.2 reveals that Robert is not malingering or intentionally overreporting symptoms. Rather, his reponse style is itself symptomatic of rather severe personality pathology.

In particular, notice that Robert's VRIN and TRIN scores indicate inconsistency in the manner in which he endorsed symptoms and that his trend is to be inconsistent in the direction of responding "True." Both L and K are below a T-score of 50, and there are no indices of random or unreliable responding on the MACI (i.e., scale VV = 0, no simultaneous elevation over a BR of 75 on scales Y and Z). Together, these results support the conclusion that Robert is inclined to answer in the affirmative when prompted with items eliciting some form of psychopathology. Moreover, the resulting profiles on the MACI and

Exhibit 6.2

Selected Psychological Test Results From Robert's Evaluation

I. MACI

VV	Reliability Index	0
X	Disclosure	85
Y	Desirability	64
Z	Debasement	100
2A	Inhibited	88
2B	Doleful	79
9	Borderline Tendency	74
B	Self-Devaluation	92
E	Peer Insecurity	103
G	Family Discord	78
H	Childhood Abuse	103
DD	Impulsive Propensity	79
FF	Depressive Affect	107

II. MMPI–A

VRIN	63		OBS	82
TRIN	82 (T)		ANX	75
F	65		ALN	70
L	46		BIZ	70
K	36		LSE	71
F-minus-K	+16		SOD	72
7	79			
8	74			
6	73			
0	70			
1	65			

III. Rorschach

R = 31	Lambda = 1.21	Constellations = DEPI
EB = 5:3.0	eb = 6:0	D = 0 Adj.D = +1
FC:CF + C = 3:1	T = 0	H = 4 AG = 3
X + % = .42	F + % = .41	WSUM6 = 17
2AB + Art + Ay = 5	Zd = −4.0	P = 8

MMPI–A are consistent with his history and clinical presentation. He is extremely paranoid and hypersensitive to criticism, and he is very pessimistic and dysphoric. The MACI elevations on MACI scales *2A* (Inhibited) and *E* (Peer Insensitivity) and MMPI–A scale *6* support these findings. Moreover, the MACI Doleful *(2B)*, Self-Devaluation *(B)*, and Depressive Affect *(FF)* elevations and MMPI–A *ANX, LSE*, and *7* elevations reveal Robert's tense and dysphoric affect. The MACI Family Discord *(G)* and Childhood Abuse *(H)* elevations are consistent with his history of abuse and the current hostility he feels toward his adoptive parents.

The Rorschach results help to confirm that Robert's overreporting is symptomatic of his pathology rather than indicative of malingering or deliberate feigning. There were no responses with dramatic content associated with gore or mutilation, he gave an above-average number of responses, and he did not provide any *INCOM* or *FABCOM* responses (see Exhibit 4.1). The high *WSUM6* was due to numerous *ALOG* responses in which Robert used strained logic to justify his responses. Moreover, the poor form quality reveals deficits in his judgment and poor perceptual accuracy that is consistent with the strained reasoning, paranoid ideation, and projective defenses he exhibited on interview.

Overall, Robert's overreporting was seen as symptomatic of weak ego functions in a decompensated and intermittently psychotic adolescent with a borderline personality structure. Instead of attempting to deliberately feign psychopathology, Robert was believed to be markedly deficient in his ability to manage and titrate his emotions. Given the level of stress he was experiencing and the shaky reality testing he displayed, Robert was encountering several symptoms and difficulties that were bona fide. He has a very poor sense of how to effectively manage pressures and demands.

SYMPTOM COACHING

The manner in which various forms of adolescent psychopathology are manifest is a function of numerous factors, including the dynamics of family relationships. Oftentimes, psychopathology may be the product of a dysfunctional family system, as when an adolescent's depression is caused by severe marital conflict between the parents. With respect to symptom coaching involving exaggeration or dissimulation, the most common family dynamic is the attempt by parents during the course of a child custody evaluation in the midst of an acrimonious divorce to encourage the children to fabricate or exaggerate problems that are "caused" by the other parent. In general, symptom coaching refers to the encouragement and guidance a parent gives to the child or adolescent to produce physical or psychological symptoms. The encouragement may be subtle or overt and can arise not only in the forensic context but in clinical settings as well.

Sanders (1995) has provided an excellent comprehensive review of the phenomenon of symptom coaching. Generally, older children and adolescents may become "coauthors" of an illness, either willingly or unwillingly, through the efforts of a parent to collude with the child in producing a false or exaggerated symptom pattern. A variety of factors contribute to the adolescent's participation, including satisfaction of dependency needs, threats to have parental love and approval withdrawn, or the fact that the fabricated illness has become a "way of life" over the course of an adolescent's life. Although the diagnosis of factitious disorder by proxy (see chap. 7 in this book) has been proposed in *DSM–IV* (American Psychiatric Association, 1994), this represents an extreme case of symptom coaching. In other instances, the collusion of a parent can maintain genuine pathology, or it can represent a disturbed attempt at coping. For example, the mother who is a victim of domestic violence may foster and encourage illness in a child to redirect the abuser's focus toward a more sympathetic subject such as the child.

A variety of factors are important in assessing the extent of collusion between parent and adolescent. The first issue is the extent to which the child is aware of the symptom coaching. Although younger children, such as those under 5 years of age, may have difficulty recognizing the influence of parental collusion, adolescents are capable of recognizing the effects of parental manipulation. However, in some rare instances such as when there is a factitious disorder by proxy, the symptom coaching may be more pervasive and less a part of the teenager's conscious awareness. Generally, however, adolescents have knowledge of the parent's collusion.

A second factor that needs to be assessed is the severity of collusion between child and parent. Sanders (1995) has outlined a continuum delineating varying degrees of collusion that fosters feigned or exaggerated symptoms in children. At the less severe end of the continuum are cases of symptom coaching that are due to naivete on the part of the adolescent. These cases involve adolescents who are not aware that their symptoms are being subtly produced by the parent. Examples of participants in naive collusion include the adolescent who is not aware that medications given by a parent are producing adverse side effects and the adolescent who believes misinformation provided by a parent. At the next level of severity in the continuum are adolescents who are aware of parental coaching and who passively accept it yet do not intentionally collude with the parent. At a more severe level of the continuum are those adolescents who actively collude with the parent to feign or induce symptoms. These cases typically involve adolescents who have lengthy histories of bizarre or unusual symptoms or illnesses and who may come to believe that the illness exists as originally described by the parent during the interview. At the most severe end of the collusion continuum are those adolescents who intentionally participate in inflicting harm on themselves. These cases are most severe and may even involve folie à deux, in which bizarre obsessional or paranoid delusional beliefs about the illness or symptoms become firmly entrenched in the adolescent. Social isolation of the teenager by the parent throughout the course of childhood renders an adolescent in these most severe cases very dependent on the parent, and delusional beliefs are readily accepted because the abusing parent has been the primary source for developing the psychological skills necessary to test reality effectively.

There are a number of reasons that a parent will attempt to coach or intentionally produce physical or psychological symptoms in the adolescent. Among the more benign reasons are overzealous attempts to be a "good parent" or misguided attempts to shelter teenagers from harm. An example of benign motives was seen in the case of a young mother who began to suspect her husband of sexually abusing their daughter after the teen began developing recurrent vaginal infections. This belief arose out of the mother's wish to protect her child combined with her response to recent local newspaper articles on how to "know if your child has been sexually abused." An evaluation and consultation with the family was sufficient to allay the mother's fears.

Other motivations on the part of a parent may not be as benign. The parent who induces or fosters symptoms in his or her adolescent may do so for pathological reasons. There may be pathological needs for sympathy, poor ego boundaries, low self-esteem, severe thought disorder, and other indications of parental psychopathology. There may also be external reasons for symptom coaching, including avoidance of marital conflict, desire to obtain child custody, desire to obtain power in relationships with professionals, or seeking monetary benefits in a pending lawsuit.

Based on case studies and her analysis of the research, Sanders (1995) offered the following tentative conclusions about symptom coaching in older children. First, when one or both parents are more active in colluding to produce symptoms, there is a greater likelihood that the family will have a more firmly entrenched and consolidated symptom picture; the factitious symptomatology is more severe. Second, when one or both parents are more active in symptom presentation, there is less likelihood that the family will report any stressors that have produced a disruptive effect on the family system. In other words, there is an avoidance of emotional issues and greater focus on somatic symptoms. Third, the more active the family is in presenting symptoms, the less likely it is that family members will seek change. Instead, the family will seek encouragement and support for the status quo, and factitious symptoms will be sustained.

The implications of these issues for assessment and treatment are significant. In general, symptom coaching is extremely difficult to identify and change. Active confrontation of the feigned symptoms is likely to result in severe resistance in the best case scenario, but a more likely response is premature termination that encourages "shopping" for a sympathetic professional. More appropriate treatment goals would include the parent and adolescent's developing alternative methods for getting needs met without resorting to symptom coaching. In less severe cases, this may simply involve educating parents and the adolescent about the adverse impact that collusion has on the adolescent's and the family's functioning. Most cases, however, cannot be treated in this manner. Long-term treatment is usually needed to prompt the adolescent to develop insight into how illlnesses or symptoms have been coached (i.e., making the naive adolescent more insightful). In more difficult cases, this may involve separating the adolescent from the family through inpatient admission and providing supportive and respectful encouragement to explore alternative ways of viewing the illness. In this way, both conjoint family interviews and separate individual sessions with the parents and adolescent are an extremely important part of the assessment and treatment approach.

In order to eliminate or reduce symptom coaching, the parent and adolescent must be able to accept an alternate story and they must develop more adaptive coping methods. One therapeutic technique that can facilitate this is selective questioning and gathering of facts. The information obtained can then be used to suggest alternative explanations. Toward this end, a team approach with more demanding cases is strongly recommended; inpatient and adolescent day treatment programs are ideal settings for implementing such multidisciplinary involvement. In this way, alliances can be built with different therapists for both the parent and adolescent. Moreover, different team members can assess the receptivity of each family member to intervention and change.

Case Example: Brooke

Brooke is a 16-year-old White girl who was admitted to an acute adolescent inpatient unit due to suicidal ideation and suspected depression. She was originally brought to the hospital by her mother after a heated argument between the two over the mother's boyfriend. Over the previous few weeks, Brooke and her mother had been quarreling over the amount of time that the mother was spending with the boyfriend. It was Brooke's contention that he was an intrusive man who did not respect others, while the mother felt that Brooke was being unrealistic in her expectations. During the most recent argument, Brooke stated that she was going to "end it all" and that her mother would no longer have to worry about her. This was unusual because Brooke had no history of suicidal threats or gestures, so the mother immediately brought her in for evaluation.

On initial evaluation, Brooke was irritable and surly, and she expressed vague suicidal intent and plans. The history was also unusual. Apparently, Brooke was born as a result of a very brief relationship that her mother had had, and Brooke never knew her father. Over the course of her childhood, she had experienced a number of strange medical conditions, including a vague childhood illness that precipitated a 2-year period of home education, a "broken" arm that was placed in a cast despite X-rays that revealed no evidence of a break (i.e., the mother threatened to sue if the arm were not placed in a cast), and an extensive medical evaluation initiated by the mother for attention deficit–hyperactivity disorder that revealed no evidence of the condition.

In addition, the recent problems between Brooke and her mother were not new. The mother had had several previous relationships with men, none of which lasted very long. Invariably, the relationships ended because of Brooke's protests, or the mother would feel that the man did not take a sufficient interest in her daughter. Records from Brooke's physicians showed that her illnesses were documented primarily on the reports of either Brooke or her mother; there was rarely solid medical evidence of true injury or illness. Subsequent investigation during interviews revealed that these illnesses were exacerbated during times when the mother was dating. As a result of this history, Brooke was at least one grade level behind in all of her subjects, and she was considering dropping out of school. There had been no prior psychiatric admissions, but there had been numerous medical hospitalizations.

Formal psychological testing was attempted with Brooke, but she refused to cooperate. Resistance to psychological testing, as opposed to medical testing, is quite common in cases where symptom coaching is present. One reason for the refusal of psychological testing is that such procedures are viewed by the parent as not addressing the "real" problem as presented in the case, which is often felt to be medical rather than psychological. Other reasons for failing to cooperate with psychological testing frequently are associated with parental fears that collusion may somehow be uncovered through the testing.

Individual interviews with Brooke and with her mother, as well as conjoint interviews, were the primary method of gathering information in this case. Interestingly, Brooke and her mother gave remarkably similar versions of the history in separate interviews. They both acknowledged that they had become rather dependent on one another. Brooke was rather self-indulgent and narcissistic, requiring excessive empathy and support from her mother; the presence of a boyfriend in her mother's life was indeed threatening to Brooke. The mother was a histrionic individual who also required excessive attention and reassurance of acceptance. She felt a need to develop other relationships but acquiesced to Brooke's demands when her daughter's protests about her dating became forceful. Moreover, the most recent boyfriend was different. With Brooke approaching college age, the mother had begun to consider the possibility that her daughter would be leaving home. Of course, this thinking was on the conscious level in that the mother had not considered the enmeshment her years of sheltering and symptom collusion had caused with Brooke. This boyfriend was the first man whom the mother actually considered as a possible long-term partner, and she was even considering marrying him. Brooke experienced this threat as too great, and a psychiatric admission resulted.

In joint interviews, Brooke and her mother presented in a markedly different way than they had during individual interviews. They each avoided addressing their enmeshment with one another and focused instead on Brooke's "depression." In fact, the clinical diagnosis was initially oppositional–defiant disorder and a borderline personality disorder. However, the mother made frequent inquiries about the possibility of a "chemical imbalance" and requested that medical testing be done to see if Brooke suffered a depressive disorder. In response to these demands, Brooke would openly complain to her mother about the "awful" conditions on the unit, and these complaints would foster further concerns by the mother about possible depression.

This case involved symptom coaching that had been ongoing for several years. It was clear that the mother was pressing the issue of depression, despite the virtual absence of clinical evidence for a depressive disturbance; Brooke exhibited no vegetative symptoms, and clinically, her mood was angry and surly rather than dysphoric. Over a period of several years, Brooke and her mother had become highly dependent on one another. Moreover, they appeared to be in a battle over whose needs for narcissistic mirroring would take precedence. For Brooke, feigned and factitious symptoms appeared to foster the mother's attention, whereas the role of an extremely diligent and concerned caretaker obtained attention and admiration from respected professionals for the mother.

The short-term goals of treatment were to resolve the issue of suicidal risk and to stabilize Brooke's affect. Toward this end, both she and the mother were educated about depression, and the evidence as to why the clinical staff believed that Brooke did not have a clinical depression was objectively presented in a "medicalized" fashion that was acceptable to both of them. Because of the emphasis on medical as opposed to psychological criteria, Brooke and her mother were able to accept the conceptualization of the crisis as a situational adjustment reaction.

On an intermediate level, the treatment goal was to encourage more mature coping with the conflict over the mother's dating. Although Brooke had difficulty accepting the mother's need for male companionship, the situation was reframed as an opportunity for Brooke to be more "grown-up" and to have more independence when the mother was with her boyfriend. The prospect of being given a more adult-like and responsible status was appealing to Brooke, given her need for control. Likewise, her mother felt empowered by the support given for her need to develop other intimate relationships.

These interventions addressed more immediate treatment goals and helped to resolve the major problems that had precipitated hospitalization. However, the long-term prognosis was extremely guarded. The enmeshment between Brooke and her mother was long-standing, and the mother's periodic symptom coaching and Brooke's collusion were a persistent problem. Fortunately, there was no evidence of severe harm to Brooke, as her mother had apparently never intentionally produced illness or injury in her daughter; nor did her mother ever deliberately administer toxic agents to induce symptoms, as is frequently seen in severe cases of factitious disorder by proxy. In adolescents, symptom coaching by parents in clinical settings is frequently part of a deeply entrenched problem that often becomes a way of life for both parent and child, and long-term change is difficult to achieve.

CONCLUSION

There are various forms of deception and manipulation of symptoms occurring in adolescent treatment settings that create challenges for the psychotherapist. One of the major problems that results from inaccurate self-reporting is that the teenage patient may be viewed as untreatable because of severe denial and resistance or as a "faker" who is taking up valuable resources in cases where there is symptom overreporting. It is crucial to avoid making preliminary judgments about adolescents in these circumstances; instead, the underlying factors that maintain the deceptive response set should be explored. Moreover, clinicians need to explore the underlying motives for an adolescent's maintaining a particular response set.

The major response sets seen in clinical settings include denial, resistance, overreporting, exaggeration, and coached symptomatology. Each of these creates unique challenges for the therapist, but specific strategies are outlined for addressing them. Reframing an adolescent's resistance or denial can reduce conflict in treatment, and conceptualizing symptom exaggeration or overreporting within a context of severe forms of pathology can be very useful. Of course, this does not eliminate the possibility that pure forms of malingering may be present in individual cases. The presence of symptom coaching can range in severity from relatively benign forms of collusion to more severe forms of enmeshment with family members. A treatment team approach is particularly useful in cases where there is severe or long-standing symptom coaching.

Malingering and deception in clinical treatment settings can become important areas of focus in treatment. However, the significance of these phenomena in forensic settings is equally great. The potential impact of the mental health professional's assessment can be far-reaching, as the next chapter will illustrate.

7

Applications in Forensic Settings

The role of a mental health professional in forensic contexts is distinctly different from that in clinical settings. Failure to acknowledge this difference can be disastrous for anyone who applies the values and roles of one to the other. As Hess (1987) outlined, there are contrasting conceptual frameworks in psychology and law. Psychologists rely on an empirical knowledge base that develops through controlled experimentation and a presumption of scientific objectivity. Legal professionals work from a rational knowledge base in which the individual case method is used within a framework of advocacy. Hess noted further that psychologists are exploratory, often examining the validity of multiple theories, with a conservative approach to accepting or rejecting hypotheses. Attorneys, on the other hand, adopt a conservative approach to theory by closely adhering to precedent and prior rulings. For attorneys, however, the criteria for resolution is expedient, because the criteria for judgment is often less stringent (e.g., preponderance of the evidence, clear and convincing proof).

Should one neglect to recognize the value differences between law and psychology, errors in the application of the behavioral sciences to legal contexts are likely to occur. For instance, in a therapeutic role, mental health professionals must develop a working alliance with individuals seeking help. The focus may be on empathic understanding and exploration of ideas, beliefs, and fantasies that have a very marginal level of validity or credibility. Although this approach may be entirely appropriate in work with adolescents who have been traumatized in some way, it is generally not appropriate for use in an assessment of causal factors in a personal injury case. When used judiciously, empathy might be a useful interviewing tool in forensic settings to obtain sensitive information. However, the goal of empathy in treatment (i.e., fostering therapeutic alliance, reducing symptom severity) is different from its use in a forensic evaluation (i.e., facilitating data collection).

Clinical work and forensic work are different from one another in many ways. Whereas a clinical goal may be the alleviation of symptoms, a forensic goal may be gathering objective data to answer a psycholegal question. In clinical settings, therapists often function as supportive advocates for the individuals they treat, but a forensic practitioner should function as an objective "scientist" who seeks facts, analyzes data, and tests hypotheses. Unfortunately, it is the blending of clinical and forensic roles that can lead to the kinds of tragic outcomes that are often found in, for example, unilateral determinations of child custody by one party's therapist or repressed memory validation with therapeutic hypnosis in personal injury cases.

Maintaining clear goals and awareness of clinical versus forensic boundaries is important to ensure that indiviudals served in these divergent settings receive the best possible service. This chapter addresses dissimulation and deception in forensic settings. The specific topics covered are voluntariness of confessions made by adolescents, malingering in criminal cases, response style concerns in juvenile status offense and transfer to adult status proceedings, and deceptive processes in cases involving factitious disorder by proxy. Again, these topics are not exhaustive, but do reflect areas of increased research and clinical interest in recent years.

VOLUNTARINESS OF CONFESSIONS

In any system of criminal justice, there is no stronger evidence that is considered by any judge or jury than the fact that a defendant has confessed to a crime. According to Wrightsman and Kassin (1993), 80% to 95% of all criminal cases never go to trial, because a defendant admits, or "confesses," to a crime by pleading guilty. Indeed, a confession is often viewed as the single most important piece of evidence that police and prosecutors can have. Therefore, great efforts are often invested in interrogating suspects with the goal of ultimately obtaining a confession.

A confession is defined as "a voluntary statement made by a person charged with the commission of a crime . . . communicated to another person, wherein he acknowledges himself to be guilty of the offense charged" (*Black's Law Dictionary*, 1990, p. 296). In some instances, confessions are broadly defined as any self-incriminating statement or behavior. For example, the infamous "white Bronco" chase initiated by O. J. Simpson just prior to his arrest on murder charges was viewed by many as an admission of guilt. The reasoning goes that because he was fleeing, he "must have been guilty." His physical behavior, rather than his verbal behavior, was seen as his "confession."

In 1966, the U.S. Supreme Court rendered its landmark case on the custodial and pretrial rights of criminal defendants in *Miranda v. Arizona* (1966). The *Miranda* opinion held that criminal suspects must be informed of their rights to maintain silence and to legal counsel before interrogation begins by police officials. Juveniles were afforded the same rights to legal counsel as adults in *In re Gault* (1967). It was not until the U.S. Supreme Court decision in *Fare v. Michael C.* (1979) that the issue of a juvenile's waiver of *Miranda* rights was decided. In *Fare*, the court held that voluntariness of a juvenile's waiver depends on the totality of the circumstances and not on a specific characteristic of the adolescent.

This development in case law on the legal rights of juveniles prompted an examination into the capacity of adolescents to waive *Miranda* rights. A large-scale study by Grisso (1980, 1981) found that younger adolescents (i.e., age 14 and younger) do not have adequate comprehension of the nature or importance of *Miranda* rights to remain silent and/or have legal counsel present during police questioning. Moreover, although older adolescents showed an understanding of *Mi-*

randa rights comparable to that of adults, the adult standard was not well suited for adolescents. Therefore, Grisso concluded from his research that teenagers cannot be considered capable of intelligently, knowingly, and voluntarily waiving their *Miranda* rights.

Prior to the decision in *Fare,* there had been other U.S. Supreme Court cases that ruled on the voluntariness of juvenile confessions in the pre-*Miranda* era. For example, in *Haley v. Ohio* (1948), the Court held that a 15-year-old could not be judged according to the same standard of maturity as an adult and was a "victim" of police interrogation procedures. The court held that a juvenile should have some adult present to assist with the stressful interrogation process. A second case, *Gallegos v. Colorado* (1962), had a similar ruling in recognizing that a 14-year-old is viewed as lacking adequate knowledge and appreciation of his or her rights and the significance of waiving them. Thus, there is sound case law that presumes that adolescents lack adequate understanding of their rights and the significance of confessing to a crime.

Even when criminal defendants are provided with adequate *Miranda* warnings, police officials can still exert pressures on a suspect in the hope of inducing a confession. Although adults are often presumed to possess sufficient control over their behavior, the police are still capable of inducing an innocent person to confess to a crime that he or she did not commit. The issue of suggestibility to interrogation has become a rapidly growing concept in psychological research (Gudjonsson, 1992; Wrightsman & Kassin, 1993).

Interrogative suggestibility is typically defined as the tendency for individuals to accept messages that are communicated during a formal questioning procedure to such an extent that the person's behavioral response is altered (Gudjonsson, 1992). Therefore, a suspect may be told during interrogation that he or she may be guilty, leading the suspect to change his or her behavior—for example, admitting to the commission of a crime that was initially denied.

The interrogative suggestibility of adolescents has also been examined in several studies. Although juveniles over the age of 12 are not any more likely than adults to succumb to leading questions during interrogation, they are significantly more likely to give in to pressures such as criticism and negative feedback when undergoing interrogation (Gudjonsson & Singh, 1984; Singh & Gudjonsson, 1992). Richardson, Gudjonsson, and Kelly (1995) found that adolescents showed a vulnerability to interrogation procedures in that they were more likely than adults to change answers they had previously given when presented with negative feedback.

The voluntariness of a confession may become the subject of dispute because a defendant claims that his or her incriminating statement is the product of coercive interrogation methods, personal needs, or some other factor that invalidates its veracity. There are many types of confessions that can arise in criminal forensic cases, as illustrated in Figure 7.1. More specifically, a confession can either be retracted, whereby the defendant recants and claims that the confession was not valid in the first place, or be nonretracted. Both retracted and nonretracted confessions may be true or false. A true retracted confession is a confession that the juvenile later claims was false, when in fact it is true; such a confession is retracted to avoid adverse treatment by the courts. A false retracted confession is one that is false and is subsequently denied by the juvenile. In such a case, an attorney may request a psychological evaluation to to aid in the defense in subsequent legal proceedings.

There are three basic types of false confessions that have been described in detail (Gudjonsson, 1992; Wrightsman & Kassin, 1993); they are indicated by the three shaded boxes in Figure 7.1. The first is *voluntary false confessions,* in which the suspect voluntarily confesses to a crime. Generally, this type of false confession is not the product of coercive police interrogation tactics and is typically given when the individual goes voluntarily to the police. A common reason that a suspect gives a voluntary false confession is to protect the identity of the actual guilty party. Thus, an older sibling may confess to protect a younger member of the family, or an adolescent may confess to protect an older peer with an extensive criminal record, who would face harsher punishment from the criminal justice system. Voluntary false confessions may also occur for reasons related to psychopathology in the defendant,

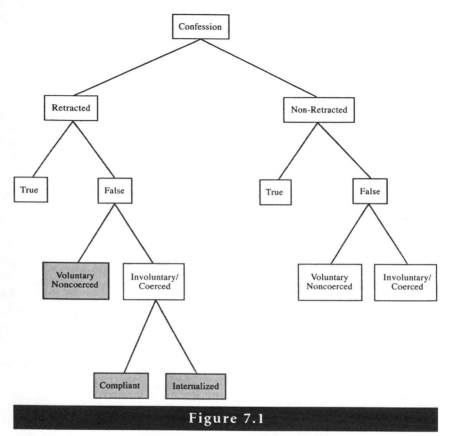

Figure 7.1

A decision tree for identifying types of confessions in criminal cases.

such as a morbid desire for notoriety, unconscious needs to punish oneself or to make amends for past offenses, and difficulty distinguishing fact from fantasy (Wrightsman & Kassin, 1993). According to research cited by Gudjonsson (1992), voluntary false confessions are reported by about 25% of all juveniles in forensic settings; the major motive in such cases is to protect the identity of the guilty party (i.e., usually an older offender or one with a prior record of violent offenses). Those who confess in order to protect the identity of the true offender are the least pathological of individuals who provide voluntary false confessions.

A second form of false confession is termed *coerced–compliant.* Confessions of this sort are typically the product of intense police interrogation methods aimed at getting a suspect to confess. Generally, coerced–compliant confessions are offered when the suspect succumbs to pressure tactics in order to "get it over with" and end an uncomfortable and emotional period of intensive questioning. Providing a confession in such cases permits an immediate escape from a stressful, tension-filled interrogation without much thought about the longer term consequences of confessing to a crime. Adolescents frequently have difficulty seeing the future implications of their behavior, and they may therefore believe that if they confess, they will be allowed to go home to their parents, avoid being locked up, or receive some other short-term benefit. Moreover, some adolescents may be more prone to "believe that somehow the truth will come out later . . . or that their [lawyer] will be able to rectify their false confession" (Gudjonsson, 1992, p. 228).

The third type of false confession is termed *coerced–internalized.* Confessions of this type are those in which a highly suggestible person comes to believe that "I must have done it, even though I don't remember." Individuals prone to give this form of false confession are among the most suggestible, and they often succumb to suggestions from police that tend to "normalize" or minimize the nature of the alleged criminal act. Coerced–internalized confessions result from a condition termed *memory distrust syndrome,* in which the individual does not trust his or her own memory of an event (Gudjonsson, 1992). The basis for one's lack of confidence in recall can be due to drug- or alcohol-induced amnesia or to the pressures exerted by interrogation. Reliance on external cues and suggestions of normality (e.g., "Anyone in the same situation would have acted that way") influences the defendant to gradually distrust his or her memory and to adopt the suggestions of others.

On the right half of the decision tree in Figure 7.1 are confessions that are not likely to be contested in legal settings, let alone be a focus of evaluation by forensic professionals, as these are nonretracted confessions. Those nonretracted confessions that are true, reflect admissions of guilt; nonretracted confessions that are false can be either voluntary or coerced. Whether the confession is voluntary or coerced, the defendant fails to retract an admission of guilt that is false. The failure to retract may be for several reasons. A young suspect may give a voluntary false confession to protect an older peer and then will not retract later for fear of retaliation, to obtain enhanced status in a gang upon release for not being a "rat," or for other self-protective reasons. Additionally, false coerced confessions may not be retracted because the suspect does not trust his or her recollection of the event and remains hopeless that a judge or jury will believe statements of denial.

The key decision in analyzing the confession of an adolescent is determining whether it is true or false. This ultimate question is often impossible to answer with complete accuracy and confidence. However, psychological assessment in cases of disputed confessions can be useful in highlighting a variety of factors that are either consistent or inconsistent with the features of a particular type of false confession. Gudjonsson (1992) lists four general factors that should be assessed in any psychological evaluation of a defendant when a dispute arises over the veracity of a confession. Exhibit 7.1 summarizes these factors into the following areas: (a) characteristics about the suspect, (b) circumstances of the arrest and custody, (c) the individual's mental and physical state during questioning, and (d) factors associated with the style of interrogation.

A variety of demographic, personality, and other psychological factors will influence an adolescent's response to police interrogation. As discussed earlier, Grisso (1980) has demonstrated that with respect to age, for example, younger juveniles do not understand the nature of their *Miranda* warnings and that they have little appreciation for the significance of waiving those rights. Even older adolescents, age 15 and 16, are typically poor at comprehending *Miranda* rights, particularly if their IQ is below 80. Psychological evaluations can also provide information about an adolescent's intellectual functioning and psychoeducational skills such as reading comprehension, verbal reasoning, problem solving, and verbal comprehension.

Many jurisdictions have preprinted sheets on which *Miranda* rights

---

Exhibit 7.1

Assessment Issues in Cases Involving Disputed Confessions

I. Defendant Characteristics
   A. Demographics (e.g., age, race, gender)
   B. Prior legal experiences (e.g., arrests, interrogations, incarcerations)
   C. Intellectual functioning
   D. Psychoeducational skills (e.g., reading level)
   E. Personality factors (e.g., suggestibility, submissiveness, oppositionality)
   F. Medical factors (e.g., medications)

II. Arrest and Custody Circumstances
   A. Timing of arrest (e.g., time of day, duration, suddenness of arrest)
   B. Voluntary vs. involuntary approach of defendant to police
   C. Timing of interrogation (e.g., number of sessions, duration)
   D. Comprehension of Miranda warnings

III. Mental State During Custody
   A. Physical evidence (e.g., written statement, videotape, affidavits, audiotapes)

IV. Interrogation Factors
   A. Style of questioning
   B. Physical layout of room
   C. Interaction of interrogator style and defendant characteristics

---

appear and have been intitialed or signed by the suspect. Copies of these forms should be obtained so that during interviews with the suspect the examiner can ask directly about the adolescent's comprehension and understanding of various components of *Miranda* warnings. Grisso (1980, 1981) has developed specialized scales for assessing comprehension and understanding of *Miranda* warnings in juveniles. These measures are useful for evaluating specific factors, such as an adolescent's understanding of the vocabulary used in warnings and the reasoning used when decisions are made involving the waiver or exercise of *Miranda* rights. Because Grisso's measures are not commerically available and are available mainly as research measures, their accessibility may be limited for some practitioners. Despite the fact that *Miranda* warnings are highly similar across jurisdictions, there may be subtle differences in wording or vocabulary. Therefore, adolescents who have signed *Miranda* sheets should be asked to define in their own words what each component of the warnings means. Likewise, specific words used (e.g., *lawyer, court of law*) can then be defined to determine the specific meaning attributed to each term by the adolescent. Oftentimes, an adolescent's prior experience (or lack thereof) with the legal system dictates his or her understanding of various aspects of *Miranda* warnings. Therefore, findings from the interview should be interpreted in light of the suspect's prior legal history.

Personality factors are another important component in an evaluation of the dynamics of adolescent confessions. Individuals who are overly submissive, conforming, or approval-seeking may be more easily influenced by external coercion and interrogative pressures, leading to a greater likelihood of coerced confessions. Therefore, personality measures (e.g., the Submissive, Conforming, and Self-Demeaning scales on the MACI) that are designed to reveal such tendencies in adolescents can be useful parts of the assessment. In the same way, personality characteristics such as oppositionality, defiance, or suspiciousness suggest characterological resistance to external coercive factors. Thus, the MACI Unruly, Oppositional, and Forceful scales and MMPI–A scales *4* and *6* may be particularly useful. In short, personality assessment is an important aspect of forensic evaluations involving disputed confessions.

The other factors outlined in Exhibit 7.1 provide extremely important and relevant variables that must be assessed in cases of this sort. There are no clear-cut decision rules about how determinative any one factor is. Sound professional judgment and conclusions that do not extend beyond the data are important guiding principles when conducting evaluations on the voluntariness of confessions. The following case example outlines findings from an extensive evaluation on an adolescent who claimed to have made a confession to a crime that he later retracted.

Case Example: Steven

Steven is an 18-year-old White youth who was referred by his attorney for a psychological evaluation in connection with a confession he provided to police. He reportedly telephoned the police station to inform them that he had witnessed a purse snatching and wanted to help the police solve the crime. When they reviewed their log and learned that earlier in the evening a woman had filed a report that her purse had been taken by a group of individuals, the police requested that Steven come to the station to provide a statement, and he agreed to do so. According to his initial statement, two acquaintances had asked Steven to go to a neighborhood bar. On the way, they started talking about needing money. One of the friends suggested that they snatch a purse, but Steven apparently refused. When one of the other friends unexpectedly took a woman's purse and ran, Steven reportedly ran to avoid getting caught.

It was Steven's contention that he went to police so that they would not think he was involved. However, when he took them to the place that his friend had allegedly dumped the empty purse and a shirt the robber wore—a piece of clothing that was later determined to belong to Steven—police began to suspect him as the perpetrator. He was taken to headquarters and interrogated for a little over 2 hours. Although he initially implicated the others, the detectives did not believe him and told him "You're not going anywhere" until he told them "the truth." Steven claimed to have a seizure disorder that required medication, so because he "wanted to go home" to get his medication, he provided a full written confession in which he admitted taking the purse. Moreover, he believed that he would be able to go home after he told police officers what they wanted to hear.

The concern about a potential false confession was raised by Steven's attorney because of a lengthy history of severe abuse and the fact that Steven had been raised in state institutions for most of his life. Steven took an anticonvulsant medication for a documented seizure disorder, and he had been in seven different psychiatric hospitals and residential treatment centers since the age of 12. He denied any history of alcohol or drug abuse, and he had never completed formal schooling past the sixth grade. He experienced flashbacks of severe physical abuse, and there was evidence of posttraumatic stress disorder. Hospital records indicated a prior diagnosis of borderline personality disorder, and Steven exhibited very aggressive and assaultive behavior when provoked. There were prior arrests for burglary, trespassing, harassment, and stalking of an ex-girlfriend. In addition to the present robbery charge, Steven was facing two counts of burglary from an unrelated incident.

Given these facts and background, if Steven's confession was indeed false, it would be classified as a coerced–compliant confession as outlined in Figure 7.1, because he was motivated to bring to a close an interrogation session that he experienced as stressful. There was no attempt to conceal the identity of some other person, as in a voluntary false confession, and Steven did not come to believe that he might have actually committed the crime as in a coerced–internalized confession.

The psychological evaluation included formal psychological testing, consisting of the WAIS–R, Wide Range Achievement Test–3 (WRAT–3), SIRS, and MCMI–III. The MCMI–III was chosen over the MACI because Steven was not in school, he was living independently, and there were diagnostic issues related to severe psychopathology that are not measured by the MACI. The testing results are presented in Exhibit 7.2. It is interesting to note that Steven functions in the borderline range of intelligence and his reading is at a grade level consistent with the last grade he had completed.

The use of a reading level is important in cases involving disputed confessions because it can provide a key piece of data when analyzing the statement. An additional analysis can also be performed on the written statement itself by typing it into a word processing program that has the capability of computing a readability statistic. Most word processing programs have this capacity; for example, WordPerfect and Word for Windows have readability analyses that can compute a Flesch Kincaid index (Flesch, 1948) or other indices of reading difficulty. Steven's written confession was found to have a readability level at the

---

Exhibit 7.2

Selected Psychological Test Results From Steven's Evaluation

I. Psychoeducational Testing

WAIS−R: Verbal IQ = 77, Performance IQ = 89, Full Scale IQ = 80

WRAT−3: Reading = 82 (sixth grade), Spelling = 84, (sixth grade), Arithmetic = 72 (fourth grade)

II. SIRS

RS	Rare Symptoms	4	Indeterminate
SC	Symptom Combination	6	Indeterminate
IA	Improbable/Absurd	2	Honest
BL	Blatant	3	Honest
SU	Subtle	11	Indeterminate
SEL	Selectivity	9	Indeterminate
SEV	Severity	5	Indeterminate
RO	Reported vs. Observed	3	Indeterminate

III. MCMI−III

V	Validity Scale	0
X	Disclosure	80
Y	Desirability	35
Z	Debasement	81
8A	Passive−Aggressive	94
1	Schizoid	90
2B	Depressive	89
3	Dependent	79
C	Borderline	81
A	Anxiety	106
R	Posttraumatic Stress	91
SS	Thought Disorder	81
D	Dysthymia	81
N	Bipolar: Manic	77

fourth grade, which is below his assessed reading level and thus within his capability.

Additionally, the data from the SIRS reveal no scales elevated in the Definite or Probable range, but six of the eight scales fall in the Indeterminate range. These results suggest that Steven is not malingering or intentionally dissimulating psychopathology, but there is some evidence of unusual responding across most scales. The MCMI–III reveals a valid profile as well, with Debasement (scale Z) below 90 and Disclosure (scale X) also below 90. However, there is a distinct tendency for Steven to overreport symptoms and to focus on the most negative aspects of his functioning. These results were interpreted as overreporting that was itself symptomatic of severe personality disturbance, but not of intentional malingering.

Steven's MCMI–III profile has some important implications for the issue of his susceptibility to succumb to interrogative pressure. In particular, his highest scale is Passive–Aggressive/Negativistic (scale $8A$) at a BR score of 94. This reflects Steven's extreme oppositionality, irritability, and angry tendencies; in short, the results suggest that Steven is not submissive, compliant, or easily influenced. On the other hand, there is also evidence of impulsivity (scales C and N) and poor judgment (scale SS) that raises the concern that he may have provided a false statement impulsively, with little thought about the potential implications of doing so.

Finally, Steven was found to be of questionable reliability on clinical interview. For example, when given a copy of his confession and asked if his signature was at the bottom, he claimed it was a forgery. This signature was found to be virtually identical to the signature he provided on the WRAT–3 when asked to write his name. When confronted with the similarity, he attempted to explain the difference between the two signature samples by focusing on very small details that were not apparent to the examiner.

Based on findings from the evaluation, some factors appeared to support Steven's claim of a false confession. He had a documented seizure disorder and required medication; he also approached the police voluntarily and did not attempt to evade them. However, several factors were present that raised serious reservations about Steven's claim of a false confession. Among the more significant factors were his ability to read the confession and understand its content, the presence of oppositional and passive–aggressive personality traits as opposed to high levels of submissiveness and suggestibility, the plausible hypothesis that he sought out police voluntarily to divert attention away from himself, and his unreliability and questionable veracity during the interview.

As a result, the ultimate finding was inconclusive, as there was no strong evidence of a false confession; Steven's confession could be valid or false, and there is no solid evidence of a coerced–compliant confession. His attorney was advised of these findings, and Steven was subsequently presented with the evidence against him. The attorney provided him with a rational analysis of the potential outcome and of any possible defense strategies and their likelihood of success. Steven withdrew his claim of false confession and decided to plead guilty to the robbery charge.

MALINGERING IN CRIMINAL CASES

An adolescent facing criminal charges is in a context that implies the presence of strong external incentives to avoid incarceration. In criminal cases where psychological evaluations are sought to answer specific questions, there is always a concern that the defendant may be feigning psychiatric illness to gain admission to a psychiatric hospital, avoid culpability through an insanity defense, or seek leniency in sentencing. The assessment for potential malingering is always a key component to any mental health evaluation in a criminal context.

The prototypic criminal case calling for psychological expertise involves the defendant who raises a defense of insanity. Most insanity statutes permit a defendant to be held not guilty of criminal conduct if a mental disease or defect interfered with the defendant's ability to know the wrongfulness of his or her conduct or the nature and consequences of the act. A few states permit a finding that the mental disease or defect prevented the defendant from conforming his or her behavior to the requirements of the law, even if he or she recognized the wrongfulness of the act. A common concern is that defendants who are not genuinely mentally ill will convincingly feign a mental disorder in order to avoid culpability.

With respect to adolescents, there are empirical data to suggest that the insanity defense is less likely to be successful than it is for adult populations. In a very comprehensive study of the insanity defense, Steadman, McGreevy, Morrissey, Callahan, Robbins, and Cirincione (1993) found that a successful insanity defense was more likely in defendants who were in their 30s. Whereas adolescents (i.e., defendants under the age of 20) represent 10% of convicted felons, there is a greater number of those adolescent defendants who were convicted when raising an insanity defense (15.2%) than those acquitted with an insanity defense (5.5%) in the four states (New York, California, Georgia, and Montana) studied by Steadman and his colleagues. When compared with data from other age groups, adolescents were the only age group in which the conviction rate for defendants raising an insanity defense was noticeably higher than the overall conviction rate for all individuals in a particular age group. That is, younger defendants in their teenage years were least likely to mount a successful insanity defense.

Cases involving the insanity defense are not the only ones in which malingering is a major concern. There are sentencing hearings, competency to stand trial proceedings, and trials where mitigating factors are presented that raise the issue of potential malingering. The following cases illustrate how assessment procedures discussed earlier can be used to answer questions pertaining to dissimulation. Other criminal proceedings may involve status offenses and juvenile transfer to adult status hearings. These topics are discussed in greater detail later in this chapter because they involve different issues that have implications for the assessment process.

Case Example: George

This case briefly illustrates how blatant attempts to feign mental illness can sometimes be identified through careful interviewing and record review. Although psychological testing was not used, this represents the exception rather than the rule; formal testing is recommended in most cases. The obvious nature of the dissimulation in this case and the nature of the question asked made psychological testing unnecessary.

George is a 16-year-old White youth who was referred for evaluation in connection with a sentencing hearing. He had previously pled guilty to burglary and had been given a sentence of intensive probation. Although he was also required to attend substance abuse treatment, George failed to appear for several appointments with his probation officer and had tested positive for cocaine and marijuana during random drug testing, resulting in his expulsion from the treatment program. He was now facing a charge of violation of probation and was going to be placed in a juvenile detention facility.

Before the hearing, George began to tell his lawyer about how "sick" he was and that he needed help. The attorney referred him for psychological evaluation to determine if there was a genuine psychiatric illness that required hospitalization. The records revealed no history of prior psychiatric treatment, and in substance abuse treatment records there was no indication of psychosis or other severe mental disorder. There was documentation of borderline intellectual functioning and long-standing learning difficulties. On interview, George presented as a very unsophisticated youth with normal affect and mood. He claimed to experience command auditory hallucinations of voices telling him, "Don't go . . . don't go to probation." Moreover, for almost every wrongful or maladaptive behavior George had ever exhibited, he claimed to have experienced a command hallucination. The context of these hallucinations had no psychodynamic significance, and they were not tied in any way to delusional thought content. The only unifying theme was that the voices told George to perform a particular act that had subsequently gotten him into trouble. In addition, George admitted that he experienced visual hallucinations in which he saw "purple horseshoes, blue moons, yellow stars, green clovers, blue diamonds . . . red hearts." His description of the visual hallucinations was taken almost verbatim from a commercial for Lucky Charms cereal. More important, George did not appear at all distressed about his hallucinations and could not identify any reason why he should try to eliminate or cope with his symptoms.

The fact that George is of limited intellectual capability helps to explain why he attempted to malinger in a rather unsophisticated and transparent fashion. It has been observed in clinical and forensic settings that unsophisticated or intellectually limited adolescents sometimes use information or material from popular media and incorporate it into their malingered presentation of feigned psychopathology. In George's case, the records and clinical interview were sufficient to answer the narrow question posed by his attorney. That is, there was no evidence of bona fide mental illness that would be a mitigating factor at the time of sentencing. Although George's substance abuse was well documented and a potential mitigating factor, the attorney stated that this issue would probably not be well received by the court because George had been in several treatment programs during the course of his probation and had not successfully completed any of them.

Case Example: Henry

In the months prior to the psychological evaluation, Henry, a 16-year-old White youth, had been burglarizing homes in his neighborhood. The nature of his criminal activity was unusual in that he broke into five different residences and stole only women's undergarments. Despite the fact that valuables such as money, jewelry, and electronic equipment were within easy reach, Henry took only the women's underwear and lingerie. He was arrested and charged with burglary after providing a full confession. Given the bizarre nature of the offenses, a psychological evaluation was requested by Henry's attorney to determine whether or not he had a viable insanity defense; treatment recommendations were also sought.

Henry had a prior history of outpatient psychological treatment for adjustment difficulties after he left his mother's home and went to live with his father. The parents had been divorced for 8 years. The history revealed average performance and no significant behavioral difficulties at school. Henry denied any substance abuse, and there were no health problems. However, there was considerable disruption in his family in that he was not treated well by his mother. She had basically ignored him his whole life, never even buying him a birthday or Christmas gift, and she acted as though Henry's two older siblings were her only children. He was encopretic until the age of 12, at which time he went to live with his father.

From the interview it was discovered that Henry had engaged in fetishistic behavior involving women's undergarments since he moved from his mother's home. He denied any history of sexual abuse and stated that the burglaries were prompted by arguments with his girlfriend after she ignored him or put him off. There was no evidence of hallucinations, delusions, or other psychotic symptoms and no signs of mood disturbance. Henry experienced periods of impulsivity and directed aggressive displays of anger at objects or property but rarely toward people. He is of average intelligence and displays no memory or other cognitive deficits.

The screening for malingering with the SIRS, MACI, and MMPI–A revealed no evidence of dissimulation or malingering. As Exhibit 7.3 illustrates, there were no SIRS scales in the Probable or Definite range, and the validity and modifier scales on the MMPI–A and MACI, respectively, are all within normal limits. Overall, the test results indicate honest responding, and this is very consistent with the observations during interviewing. Henry was open and frank about his behavior, and he was not at all defensive or guarded. Nevertheless, he had limited insight into the exact motive for his behavior, but this was seen as the manifestation of psychological defenses and a focus for treatment, rather than deliberate evasiveness or denial.

The attorney was informed that in the opinion of the examiner, there was no evidence of a viable insanity defense. Henry clearly made efforts to conceal his activity by burglarizing the homes when people were away or in the early morning hours, and he was aware of the consequences and nature of his actions. More significantly, he did not present with a serious mental disease or defect. There were positive indicators for treatment, including his supportive father, average intelligence, expressed motivation for treatment, and the lack of substance abuse or serious psychopathology other than his fetish and a suspected personality disorder. These factors were presented to the attorney for possible use at a disposition/sentencing hearing.

Exhibit 7.3

Selected Psychological Test Results From Henry's Evaluation

I. MACI

VV	Reliability	0
X	Disclosure	60
Y	Desirability	56
Z	Debasement	70

II. MMPI–A

VRIN	42
TRIN	51
F	45
L	59
K	53
F-minus-K	−9

III. SIRS

RS	Rare Symptoms	0	Honest
SC	Symptom Combination	2	Honest
IA	Improbable/Absurd	0	Honest
BL	Blatant	4	Honest
SU	Subtle	11	Indeterminate
SEL	Selectivity	11	Indeterminate
SEV	Severity	4	Indeterminate
RO	Reported vs. Observed	0	Honest

FACTITIOUS DISORDER BY PROXY

Over the past several decades, society has placed great emphasis on child welfare and protecting children from abuse. One of the more recent phenomena capturing interest among professionals concerned with child welfare is Munchausen Syndrome by Proxy (Meadow, 1977, 1995). The importance of this very disturbing syndrome is evident from its entrance under the name Factitious Disorder by Proxy (FDP) into the provisional criteria sets provided for further study in the *DSM–IV* (American Psychiatric Association, 1994). The major features of FDP are (a) the intentional production or feigning of physical or psychological symptoms in an individual (usually a child) who is being cared for by another individual (usually a parent), (b) the perpetrator's motivation of assuming the sick role by proxy (i.e., through the identified patient's illness), and (c) the lack of external incentives. Therefore, a typical case of FDP involves a parent administering medications or other chemical substances to a child, thereby inducing iatrogenic illness and then adopting the role of a concerned and sympathetic parent of a sick child. A number of motives may underlie the perpetrator's dangerous and harmful behavior. Strong needs for sympathy from others and for close working relationships with persons in authority (i.e., physicians), delusional beliefs, and enhanced feelings of competence in the face of crises are among the disturbed dynamics of the FDP perpetrator.

By its very nature, FDP involves deception on the part of several different individuals. The primary caregiver clearly is deceptive in the way he or she reports or induces symptoms, and any accusations or suspicions are apt to be vigorously denied. Other adult caregivers or family members who are not responsible for inducing symptoms may still deny or minimize the behavior of the perpetrator in an effort to avoid outside intervention. The child or adolescent victim of FDP will become an unwitting accomplice in the self-report of induced symptoms. Even physicians and other service providers may deny, rationalize, or in some other way ignore the unusual behavior of a parent who induces severe and sometimes lethal illnesses in his or her child. The range of deception can indeed be pervasive in FDP cases. Because this book focuses on the evaluation of deception in adolescents, the discussion that follows is focused on teenagers; however, these comments may also apply to younger children as well. Given the nature of this syndrome, FDP has many familial dynamics and requires that attention be paid to the ways in which all individuals react, including all family members and relevant professionals involved (Alexander, 1995).

As with most psychological or psychiatric disorders, the presentation of FDP is rather diverse, and cases often differ from one another despite common dynamics and features. Rosenberg (1995) noted that although the defining feature of FDP is falsification of medical illness in a child by a caregiver, there are also persistent complaints by the offending caregiver that the true cause of the illness has not been found. Thus, it is common for the parent to question the skill and competence of professionals when they fail to satisfy the parent's needs or wishes. Moreover, Rosenberg (1995) noted that the illness can be simulated via false reporting of symptoms, intentionally produced by administering a toxic agent, or the result of a combination of these types of manipulation. Verbal deception in FDP cases occurs when a parent deliberately feigns or lies about a child's symptoms without necessarily doing anything to the child. Behavioral deception occurs when a parent deliberately inflicts some malady upon the child (e.g., administering symptom-producing drugs, breaking bones) to bring about genuine physical symptoms or conditions. The range of deceptive behavior can be extremely wide and includes deliberately withholding treatment, demanding expensive medical tests with adverse side effects under threat of a malpractice suit, and other behaviors that bring about a child's physical symptoms.

The parent's abusive deception can have profound detrimental effects ranging from recurrent illness to death. Adolescent victims of FDP frequently agree with the symptoms reported by the parent, but Rosenberg (1995) is quick to note that teenagers should not be viewed as deceptive in the same way as the adult perpetrator. The course of FDP frequently begins in childhood, and victims are often exposed to medical procedures over long periods of time, sometimes spanning years. As a result, the child learns about symptoms based on what he or she is told by a trusted adult, usually the parent. As the child enters adolescence, his or her view of recurrent illnesses is often deeply influenced by what he or she has been told over the years. Adolescent victims of FDP may collude with the parent because it is the only way of life known (Sanders, 1995). Therefore, the "deception" displayed by adolescent victims may not always be true deception. Their self-reports of symptoms can be genuine when the illness has been produced by the caregiver. In cases of simulated symptoms based on parents' self-reports, a child or adolescent will report symptoms based on what he or she believes to be true. Therefore, the adolescent's self-reports may be objectively false in the sense that the symptoms are simulated, but the intent is not to deceive but merely to report what is believed to be true. Recall from chapter 2 that the speaker's intent is a very important factor in distinguishing true statements from mistaken beliefs, misperceptions, and intentional lies. In FDP, the adolescent victim's "deception" typically consists of true statements in cases of produced symptoms and mistaken beliefs or misperceptions in cases of simulated illness due to symptom coaching by the parent.

In more severe cases, the dependent adolescent may be extremely impressionable and readily adopts the beliefs and attitudes of an enmeshed and overbearing parent (Sanders, 1995). Because the family system that has this dynamic tends to be isolated from the outside world, the adolescent may have very little opportunity for adequate reality testing outside of the family. It is not uncommon to find that over their life course, victims of FDP have changed schools frequently or have been kept out of school entirely and remain at home due to severe medical problems, thus preventing adequate development of peer relationships. This deficiency only serves to isolate the adolescent further from others and to foster extreme closeness and dependency on the parent. In more severe cases, the adolescent may develop a folie à deux, in which a delusional belief is shared with the parent about the child's illness.

The assessment of FDP cases in forensic settings demands a great deal of diligence in obtaining information from a number of different sources. An important first step is conducting thorough clinical and diagnostic interviews with the parents and adolescent, both separately and conjointly. In this way, inconsistencies in presentation may be identified to raise questions for further exploration. A second, yet equally important step is to obtain collateral information and documentation from as many sources as possible. The names of all physicians seen by the child and the dates of service should be sought so that medical records can be reviewed. It is important to note that parents may withhold the names of some physicians, particularly if they have not been viewed as supportive or helpful by the parent. However, medical records are extremely valuable in documenting the nature and extent of medical treatment and the opinions of the treating physician. School records are also crucial for documenting the adolescent's functioning outside of the home. In short, collateral records and documents are as important as the direct clinical interview.

Psychological testing can also be an important part of the forensic examination and should be considered for both the adolescent and the parent. However, actual practice in these cases has revealed a significant degree of resistance to attempts at psychological testing. The parent is usually searching for medical, as opposed to psychological, explanations, and the need for testing of the parent is seen as irrelevant. Moreover, many FDP cases are difficult to identify and often require months or years of involvement with the medical and child welfare systems before a definitive diagnosis can be made. If the case has been adjudicated, then a court order may be useful in ordering appropriate psychological evaluations. In early phases when the diagnosis of FDP is suspected, efforts to perform psychological testing may be thwarted by the parent.

The following case illustrates some of the complexities in this form of child abuse in an adolescent with a long history of strange medical problems. Moreover, it illustrates the many difficulties that arise in trying to identify and assess the FDP patient, particularly because of protective familial dynamics.

Case Example: Jeremy

A 13-year-old White youth was initially referred by the county Department of Social Services for an evaluation after two child protection reports were filed when the boy appeared at school with bruises on his face. Jeremy was a sixth-grade student who had been in special education classes throughout most of his schooling. Initially, there were concerns raised that he might have been subjected to physical abuse by his father, but the evaluation uncovered evidence of serious psychopathology and extreme enmeshment between Jeremy and his mother.

A mental health evaluation was requested to make appropriate treatment recommendations. The referring social service agency was concerned about possible FDP because Jeremy's mother had made numerous requests of her health insurance provider for approval of unusual and expensive medical tests for a seizure disorder that Jeremy allegedly had.

The preliminary interviews revealed that Jeremy had changed school districts five times in the 8 years since he had begun school. Each of these changes was prompted by the mother's dissatisfaction with the school personnel's response to her frequent complaints. For example, on one occasion, some peers allegedly punched and kicked Jeremy in the genitals. When the mother complained that these incidents of "sexual abuse" were not being handled properly, she withdrew Jeremy from the school and placed him in another school district. The investigation performed by school officials concluded that this alleged incident had never occurred.

There was also a history of numerous physical and medical problems, some of which were bizarre. These problems began in infancy when Jeremy had episodes of violent vomiting, and in early childhood, he was found to be hypoglycemic after lapsing into a coma. Following this incident, Jeremy's mother monitored his blood sugar levels on a daily basis, despite a pediatrician's opinion that no monitoring was needed. Jeremy also had frequent bouts of diarrhea and constipation, requiring his mother to give him regular enemas. Significant periods of school were missed because of recurrent medical problems; these prolonged absences caused Jeremy to fall 2 years behind in his grade level.

Complicating the assessment was the fact that Jeremy presented as highly disturbed during the clinical interview. His physical appearance was more like that of a child of 8 than that of a 13-year-old. In adolescent FDP cases, such a physical presentation is not uncommon, due to parental efforts to infantilize and shelter the teenager from growth and maturation. According to the mother, Jeremy engaged in self-injurious and self-mutilating behavior in that he would often bite himself or sit on a hot radiator when angry. His expressive speech was likewise immature, and his moods were highly variable, ranging from dysphoria and pessimism to dramatic displays of somatic difficulties and active solicitation of sympathy and concern from the examiner (e.g., lying down and placing his head in the examiner's lap during family interviews). Jeremy also reported passive suicidal ideation and vague auditory hallucinations of voices representing peers at school who were tormenting and teasing him. During the interview, he exhibited some loosening of associations, dramatic and labile affect, and perseveration in his thinking. The familial relationships were highly polarized, with the mother overly concerned about Jeremy and the father frustrated with the extreme turmoil at home. During family interviews, the mother was tearful and needy but became hostile and abrupt when her husband made efforts to comfort her.

Given Jeremy's severe emotional and behavioral dyscontrol, a recommendation for acute inpatient psychiatric treatment was made. At this time, a diagnosis of FDP could not be made because of the limited information available. Formal psychological testing was deferred because of Jeremy's severely decompensated state; it was felt that diagnostic testing would be most useful if it were conducted in the hospital and after Jeremy was both psychiatrically stabilized and temporarily separated from the family.

As is common in FDP cases, the diagnosis became clearer only after the family was able to be monitored over the course of several months. Unfortunately, such long periods of time create a risk of severe harm to the adolescent if the intentional production of symptoms becomes very intrusive. This case illustrates how tragic the results can be.

After the initial consultation, Jeremy's case was followed through ongoing consultation with the Department of Social Services. Initially, the mother reluctantly agreed to have Jeremy admitted to a psychiatric hospital, but she signed him out against medical advice within days of his admission. She then took him home, but the case worker cautioned her that failure to obtain adequate psychiatric care might result in charges of parental neglect. This issue was set aside when Jeremy began experiencing more frequent "seizures" and was medically hospitalized due to a rather severe decline in his physical health. In the hospital, the mother was observed to be attentive, although she was suspected of administering strange "herbal remedies" to Jeremy when the staff was at a distance. Throughout the course of Jeremy's hospitalization, the mother had tried to convince medical professionals of the success of various unconventional treatments. While in the hospital, Jeremy unexpectedly lapsed into a coma and died several weeks later. The official cause of death was ruled to be respiratory failure secondary to neurological illness. However, an exact neurological diagnosis was never conclusively made, and the cause of Jeremy's seizures was never found.

Two physicians treating Jeremy strongly suspected that the mother's mysterious herbal remedies consisted of toxic agents that were being administered over the course of several months. Moreover, they strongly suspected factitious illness by proxy. However, the physician in charge of the medical case was a noted specialist who at the time of Jeremy's death was "outraged" at the suggestion of factitious illness. Efforts to obtain medical records surrounding Jeremy's illness and death were thwarted. No formal abuse or neglect charges could be filed against the mother due to the lack of evidence; the social services department was unable to conclude its investigation.

At this writing, the mother had begun to make requests of social services for approval of payments for expensive and unusual medical tests for Jeremy's younger brother. This child had reportedly been in good health until Jeremy's death, at which time he began experiencing medical problems. The Department of Social Services currently has no legal basis to intervene, but as of this writing, they are monitoring the case.

STATUS OFFENSE EVALUATION

Expert testimony by mental health professionals is a very important and influential part of the adjudication process for adolescents (Melton et al., 1987). One of the major reasons for such emphasis on expert testimony is that the juvenile justice system places greater emphasis on rehabilitation and treatment than does the adult criminal justice system. Those juvenile offenders who are viewed as "hardened criminals" with little chance for reform are frequently transferred to adult courts and prosecuted as adult offenders.

Another major difference between the adult and juvenile systems is that there are far greater limits and restrictions placed on the rights of juveniles. Some of the restrictions that are instituted against teenagers are not found anywhere else in our system of justice. Consequently, many states have legislation allowing certain forms of behavior to be proscribed for juveniles based solely on their status as members of a particular age group (Mnookin & Weisberg, 1989). More specifically, certain forms of conduct (e.g., breaking curfew, defying parents or school personnel, running away from home, truancy, associating with the "wrong crowd") can be prohibited for juveniles because the conduct is viewed by the legal system as potentially harmful to the development of children and adolescents as productive members of society. As long as adults do not violate some criminal statute or other legal mandate, they cannot be legally forced to behave in certain ways such as attending work, adhering to a curfew, obeying family members, associating with a defined group of people, or following a certain set of behavioral rules.

Because of their special status in the eyes of the law, juveniles are subjected to a set of offenses known as *status offenses*, which classify the aforementioned behaviors as illegal. The nature of these offenses differs from state to state, and laws governing status offenses are often referred to as Person in Need of Supervision (PINS), Child in Need of Supervision (CINS, CHINS), or some similarly named offense.

In many cases, status offenses begin when a parent, school official, or some other interested person in authority petitions a juvenile or family court to grant an order prohibiting certain behaviors and prescribing other behaviors. Invariably, a court will impose a probationary sentence according to which a juvenile is ordered to conform his or her behavior to a legally defined set of standards. The intent is to avert more serious intervention. For instance, a judge may order the juvenile to comply with a curfew, refrain from associating with certain individuals or groups, attend school regularly, participate in treatment, or refrain from abusing substances. If the teenager violates conditions of the order, more severe interventions may ensue, including temporary placement in foster care, incarceration, or permanent placement outside the home.

At various times, forensic practitioners may be called on to evaluate a juvenile involved in status offense proceedings. Many types of diagnostic and treatment-related questions may be asked as part of the evaluation. Exhibit 7.4 presents those questions that are most frequently asked, although the list is by no means exhaustive. The first major area that can be evaluated includes treatment and rehabilitation potential, such as the need for specific types of treatment (e.g., substance abuse) or the best treatment setting (e.g., inpatient vs. outpatient) for the adolescent. Other factors that can be assessed include risk assessment, such as an adolescent's risk for suicide, violence, aggression, or recidivism. Assessment of familial and social support systems and the emotional and psychological stability of the adolescent are also important areas of concern. Many of these issues can help the court make a determi-

---

Exhibit 7.4

Issues in Status Offense and Transfer to Adult Status Evaluations

I. Treatment/Rehabilitation Potential
   A. Need for substance abuse treatment
   B. Inpatient vs. outpatient treatment setting
   C. Specific treatment recommendations
   D. Criminal justice vs. mental health setting placement
II. Risk Assessment
   A. Suicide risk/potential
   B. Violence or risk of danger to others
   C. Risk of reoffending
III. Assessment of Family/Social Environment
   A. Stability/cohesiveness of family
   B. Ability to benefit from supports and parental limits
IV. Emotional Maturity Level of Juvenile
   A. Level of insight into current behavior
   B. Capacity to make own decisions

nation about the level of restriction that an adolescent should have on his or her behavior and the type of treatment needed.

Status offense evaluations may uncover deception on the part of the adolescent or, in some cases, the family system. Adolescents charged with status offenses deny wrongdoing in an effort to avoid having restrictions placed on their freedom and rights; at other times, they may attempt to appear well adjusted to convince others of their potential for rehabilitation. Moreover, when charged with violation of probation, adolescents often deny problem areas in an attempt to convince the examiner or courts that there is no need for treatment and that returning home will result in continued stability. Of course, these efforts at minimization and denial conceal psychological problems and dysfunction in the teenager's social environment. Sometimes parents or caregivers may feel forced into a defensive posture, providing biased and deceptive reports to the court to prevent their child from being removed from the home. Other parents may exaggerate or negatively distort the adolescent's behavior in an effort to have them placed elsewhere. Henry's case example related earlier illustrates some of the issues that may be a focus in status offense evaluations.

TRANSFER TO ADULT STATUS

As previously noted, there are some adolescent offenders whose criminal history is so extensive or whose criminal behavior so outrageous that the rehabilitative focus of the juvenile justice system is overridden by the need to severely punish the offender. Therefore, some adolescents who commit a criminal act are transferred to adult status and prosecuted as adults. The major reason for transfer to adult status is that the adult criminal justice system is believed to be better equipped to administer punishment because adult sentences are more severe.

Many states have provisions that prescribe how and when an adolescent criminal defendant should be transferred to adult court. There is typically a hearing in which evidence is presented to help the court determine if transfer should be made. The prosecutor generally argues that transfer is appropriate when there is evidence of a long criminal record, severe threat to the community, or other factors pointing to the need for lengthy incarceration. Defense attorneys typically argue against transfer, based on evidence of an adolescent's rehabilitative potential, family issues (e.g., history of severe abuse), and other mitigating factors. Despite their divergent interests in a case, both prosecution and defense arguments rest on the assumption that justice is best served by either transfer to adult status or by keeping the adolescent within the juvenile justice system; that is, the legal test for transfer is what best serves the interests of justice.

The use of expert mental health testimony is an important part of the proceedings that determine whether or not transfer occurs. In particular, the factors that are relevant to status offense evaluations are also relevant in transfer proceedings. Therefore, Exhibit 7.4 can be used as a guideline for assessment. However, practitioners should be aware that transfer proceedings represent a different context than that of status offense hearings. The criminal activity of the defendant is more severe in transfer cases, and an expert's findings can have a profound impact on the adolescent's future, because the alternative to placement in a rehabilitative juvenile facility is an adult sentence. The end result for an adolescent tried as an adult may be lengthy incarceration in a correctional facility or even the death penalty for older adolescents in those states permitting capital punishment.

CONCLUSION

The application of findings from mental health evaluations to forensic settings requires an objective and neutral stance. There are a number of issues raised in legal settings where mental health professionals are called on to provide insight and direction. Although the potential range of issues evaluated in forensic settings is broad, nearly all assessments are concerned at some level with the possible presence of malingering or other forms of deception.

In this chapter, attention has been given to some of the more significant types of assessments that mental health professionals are asked to conduct, including voluntariness of confessions, criminal proceedings, FDP, status offense proceedings, and transfer to adult status hearings. Specific guidelines are offered for conducting assessments in each of these areas. Forensic practitioners must provide documentation that supports their findings; as such, the multimethod approach emphasized throughout this book can provide practitioners with the methods to conduct forensic evaluations in a comprehensive fashion. The case examples given in this chapter illustrate some of the issues that professionals typically encounter in evaluations of this sort. It is important to attend to professional standards, ethical principles, and available research findings to guide one's evaluation. The conclusions that the practitioner draws should follow from the methodology used, and they should not extend beyond the data available.

Afterword

There are many different approaches to solving problems. One approach may attempt to simplify complex matters by imposing succinct rules, whereas another may attempt to illustrate the complex nature of matters that appear at first glance to be rather simple. In the area of credibility assessment, both of these approaches have their supporters and detractors. On the one hand, those who ask a mental health professional to consult may want a simple answer to such questions as "Is this person malingering or not?" or "Do you think this person is telling the truth?" Unfortunately, there are no simple rules or guidelines one can use to answer such questions. As noted in the preface of this book, the private nature of personal thoughts, intent, and motivations generally precludes one from knowing with absolute certainty whether or not someone is being truthful.

An important point that should be recognized when mental health professionals evaluate malingering and deception is that there are no simple dichotomies. In other words, malingering, denial, and all forms of deception fall along a continuum between intentional malingering at one end and intentional denial at the other end, with honesty falling somewhere in between. At various points along this continuum lie several important variants of deception, such as unintentional symptom exaggeration secondary to severe psychopathology; acquiescent responding, which involves an individual's endorsement of a number of symptoms due to mental confusion; and varying levels of intentional and unintentional self-deception.

In this book, I have attempted to lay out the most useful and practical strategies for identifying malingering and deception in both clinical and forensic settings. One of the themes that has been repeated across various sections of the text is that no single psychological test, interview finding, or clinical observation can stand alone as a definitive indicator of malingering or deception. The final conclusion that a clinician draws in any individual case must be based on an integration of many different pieces of data. Of equal importance is the fact that the clinician must also have an appreciation for how one's findings and conclusions are to be used, especially with respect to the credibility of an adolescent. In particular, a finding of malingering can have profound implications for the teenager in that it may result in the refusal of services in clinical settings or lead to lengthy incarceration in criminal justice settings. A false positive finding (i.e., incorrectly identifying an adolescent with bona fide pathology as malingering or feigning) can have profound adverse consequences such as the denial of needed mental health services. Therefore, assessments of malingering and deception should not be approached lightly, and they should not be conducted in a cursory manner. A thorough review of the history, interviewing of the adolescent and collateral sources, and appropriate psychological testing are generally the basic necessary components to any psychological evaluation involving a question of malingering or deception.

There is a long tradition in psychological literature to note that "more research is needed" whenever the implications of one's empirical findings are discussed or clinical and theoretical issues are reviewed. With respect to the issue of adolescent malingering and deception, there is no denying the fact that there has not been very much research; there are many more questions than answers at this time. I would therefore like to close with a brief overview of some of the areas where I believe research can provide information that will be of great value to practitioners in the future. Moreover, it is my hope that this book will serve to guide not only practitioners who conduct psychological evaluations of adolescents but also researchers who wish to know more about the types of issues that will be of practical significance.

One important area that needs to be explored is the use of specific psychological assessment instruments in the evaluation of adolescent malingering and dissimulation. More specifically, the SIRS is a very important technique that has been shown to have utility in adolescent populations. However, more research is needed to examine the utility of this instrument in discriminating between malingering and genuine psychopathology of various forms. The use of known, suspected, coached, and uncoached adolescent malingerers would be very helpful. Moreover, clear decision rules for identifying indeterminate, probable, and definite malingering profiles on the SIRS are needed. Additionally, the MACI is an important instrument in the assessment of adolescent psychopathology, but it has not been the focus of any empirical research on identifying adolescent self-report styles. The MACI has several advantages over the MMPI–A that make it very useful in adolescent populations. It is recommended that efforts be undertaken to investigate the MACI's capacity for identifying biased self-report styles in the same way that the MMPI–A has been examined. Additional research is also needed in the area of identifying deception with statement reality analysis and malingering on neuropsychological testing instruments among adolescent populations.

Another important area of needed investigation is the prevalence rates of various forms of deception among adolescent populations. For instance, it makes intuitive sense that the rate of malingering, denial, honest responding, or some other response style will differ across various clinical (e.g., inpatient vs. outpatient) settings and between clinical versus forensic settings. Therefore, research is needed to identify the frequency with which the various forms of deception discussed in this book occur.

There are other important issues that need to be resolved as well. For instance, it would be extremely useful to have empirical data that can help the clinician differentiate between the adolescent who is malingering and the one who presents on psychological testing as a malingerer but who is exaggerating or overreporting symptoms as the result of poor psychological controls, severe emotional disturbance, or severe psychopathology.

The research possibilities in the area of adolescent malingering and deception are indeed great. As more is learned about the various ways in which adolescents attempt to dissimulate, the ability of the mental health professional to identify the various forms of dissimulation will improve. While clinicians await the findings yet to be discovered, it is hoped that this book will facilitate the complex and important task of credibility assessment among adolescents in both clinical and forensic settings.

References

Achenbach, T. M. (1985). *Assessment and taxonomy of child and adolescent psychopathology.* Beverly Hills, CA: Sage.

Achenbach, T. M., & Edelbrock, C. S. (1981). Behavioral problems and competencies reported by parents of normal and disturbed children aged 4 through 16. *Monographs of the Society for Research in Child Development, 46,* 1–82.

Albert, S., Fox, H. M., & Kahn, M. W. (1980). Faking psychosis on the Rorschach: Can expert judges detect malingering? *Journal of Personality Assessment, 44,* 115–119.

Alexander, R. (1995). The Munchausen syndrome by proxy family. In A. V. Levin & M. S. Sheridan (Eds.), *Munchausen syndrome by proxy: Issues in diagnosis and treatment* (pp. 59–68). Lexington, MA: Lexington Books.

Ambrosini, P. J. (1992). *Schedule for Affective Disorders and Schizophrenia for School Age Children (6–18 years): Kiddie–SADS (K–SADS).* Philadelphia: Medical College of Pennsylvania.

American Psychiatric Association. (1994). *Diagnostic and statistical manual of mental disorders* (4th ed.). Washington, DC: Author.

American Psychological Association. (1992). Ethical principles of psychologists and code of conduct. *American Psychologist, 47,* 1597–1611.

Anson, D. A., Golding, S. L., & Gully, K. J. (1993). Child sexual abuse allegations: Reliability of criteria-based content analysis. *Law & Human Behavior, 17,* 331–341.

Arbisi, P. A., & Ben-Porath, Y. S. (1995). An MMPI–2 infrequent response scale for use with psychopathological populations: The infrequency–psychopathology scale, $F(p)$ scale. *Psychological Assessment, 7,* 424–431.

Archer, R. P. (1984). Use of the MMPI with adolescents: A review of salient issues. *Clinical Psychology Review, 4,* 241–251.

Archer, R. P. (1987). *Using the MMPI with adolescents.* Hillsdale, NJ: Erlbaum.

Archer, R. P. (1992). *MMPI–A: Assessing adolescent psychopathology.* Hillsdale, NJ: Erlbaum.

Archer, R. P., & Ball, J. D. (1988). Issues in the assessment of adolescent psychopathology. In R. L. Greene (Ed.), *The MMPI: Use with specific populations* (pp. 259–277). Philadelphia: Grune & Stratton.

Archer, R. P., Gordon, R. A., & Kirchner, F. H. (1987). MMPI response-set characteristics among adolescents. *Journal of Personality Assessment, 51,* 506–516.

Archer, R. P., & Jacobson, J. M. (1993). Are critical items "critical" for the MMPI–A? *Journal of Personality Assessment, 61,* 547–556.

Archer, R. P., Maruish, M., Imhof, E. A., & Piotrowski, C. (1991). Psychological test usage with adolescent clients: 1990 survey findings. *Professional Psychology: Research and Practice, 22,* 247–252.

Ash, P., & Guyer, M. J. (1991). Biased reporting by parents undergoing child custody evaluations. *Journal of the American Academy of Child & Adolescent Psychiatry, 30,* 835–838.

Bagby, R. M., Gillis, J. R., & Rogers, R. (1991). Effectiveness of the Millon Clinical Multiaxial Inventory validity index in the detection of random responding. *Psychological Assessment, 3,* 285–287.

Baldessarini, R. J., Finkelstein, S., & Arana, G. W. (1983). The predictive power of diagnostic tests and the effect of prevalence of illness. *Archives of General Psychiatry, 40,* 569–573.

Barbaree, H. E., & Cortoni, F. A. (1993). Treatment of the juvenile sex offender within the criminal justice and mental health systems. In H. E. Barbaree, W. L. Marshall, & S. M. Hudson (Eds.), *The juvenile sex offender* (pp. 243–263). New York: Guilford Press.

Bash, I. Y., & Alpert, M. (1980). The determination of malingering. *Annals of the New York Academy of Sciences, 347,* 86–99.

Behar, L. (1977). The preschool behavior questionnaire. *Journal of Abnormal Child Psychology, 5,* 265–275.

Bekerian, D. A., & Dennett, J. L. (1995). Assessing the truth in children's statements. In T. Ney (Ed.), *True and false allegations of child sexual abuse: Assessment and case management* (pp. 163–175). New York: Brunner/Mazel.

Ben-Porath, Y. (1994). The ethical dilemma of coached malingering research. *Psychological Assessment, 6,* 14–15.

Berry, D. T. R., Lamb, D. G., Wetter, M. W., Baer, R. A., & Widiger, T. A. (1994). Ethical considerations in research on coached malingering. *Psychological Assessment, 6,* 16–17.

Bigler, E. D. (1990). Neuropsychology and malingering: Comment on Faust, Hart, and Guilemette (1988). *Journal of Consulting and Clinical Psychology, 58,* 244–247.

Black's law dictionary (6th ed.). (1990). St. Paul, MN: West.

Bourg, S., Connor, E. J., & Landis, E. E. (1995). The impact of expertise and sufficient information on psychologists' ability to detect malingering. *Behavioral Sciences & the Law, 13,* 505–515.

Brinkman, D. C., Overholser, J. C., & Klier, D. (1994). Emotional distress in adolescent psychiatric inpatients: Direct and indirect measures. *Journal of Personality Assessment, 62,* 472–484.

Bruhn, A. R., & Reed, M. R. (1975). Simulation of brain damage on the Bender-Gestalt test by college subjects. *Journal of Personality Assessment, 39,* 244–255.

Butcher, J. N., & Williams, C. L. (1992). *Essentials of MMPI–2 and MMPI–A interpretation.* Minneapolis, MN: University of Minnesota Press.

Butcher, J. N., Williams, C. L., Graham, J. R., Archer, R., Tellegen, A., Ben-Porath, Y. S., & Kaemmer, B. (1992). *MMPI–A manual for administration, scoring, and interpretation.* Minneapolis, MN: University of Minnesota Press.

Carp, A. L., & Shavzin, A. R. (1950). The susceptibility to falsification of the Rorschach psychodiagnostic technique. *Journal of Consulting Psychology, 14,* 230–233.

Ceci, S. J., & Bruck, M. (1993). The suggestibility of the child witness: A historical review and synthesis. *Psychological Bulletin, 113,* 403–439.

Ceci, S. J., & Bruck, M. (1995). *Jeopardy in the courtroom: A scientific analysis of children's testimony.* Washington, DC: American Psychological Association.

Cleckley, H. (1976). *The mask of sanity* (5th ed.). St. Louis, MO: Mosley.

Coleman, J. C. (1992). The nature of adolescence. In J. C. Coleman & C. Warren-Adamson (Eds.), *Youth policy in the 1990's: The way forward* (pp. 8–27). London: Routledge.

Committee on Ethical Guidelines for Forensic Psychologists. (1991). Specialty guidelines for forensic psychologists. *Law and Human Behavior, 15,* 655–665.

Cornell, D. G., & Hawk, G. L. (1989). Clinical presentation of malingerers diagnosed by experienced forensic psychologists. *Law and Human Behavior, 13,* 375–383.

Cullum, C. M., Heaton, R. K., & Grant, I. (1991). Psychogenic factors influencing neuropsychological performance: Somatoform disorders, factitious disorders, and malingering. In H. O. Doerr & A. S. Carlin (Eds.), *Forensic neuropsychology: Legal and scientific bases* (pp. 141–171). New York: Guilford Press.

Cunnien, A. J. (1988). Psychiatric and medical syndromes associated with deception. In R. Rogers (Ed.), *Clinical assessment of malingering and deception* (pp. 13–33). New York: Guilford Press.

Dannenbaum, S. E., & Lanyon, R. I. (1993). The use of subtle items in detecting deception. *Journal of Personality Assessment, 61,* 501–510.

Daubert v. Merrill Dow Pharmaceuticals, 113 S.Ct. 2786 (1993).

Dawes, R. M. (1995). *House of cards: Psychology and psychotherapy built on myth.* New York: Free Press.

DePaulo, B., & Jordan, A. (1982). Age changes in deceiving and detecting deceit. In R. S. Feldman (Ed.), *Development of nonverbal behavior in children* (pp. 150–180). New York: Springer.

Depaulo, B. M., Jordan, A., Irvine, A., & Laser, P. S. (1982). Age changes in the detection of deception. *Child Development, 53,* 701–709.

Ekman, P. (1985). *Telling lies: Clues to deceit in the marketplace, politics, and marriage.* New York: Norton.

Ekman, P. (1989). *Why kids lie.* New York: Penguin.

Ekman, P., Roper, G., & Hager, J. C. (1980). Deliberate facial movement. *Child Development, 51,* 886–891.

Exner, J. E. (1991). *The Rorschach: A comprehensive system: Vol. 2. Interpretation* (2nd ed.). New York: Wiley.

Exner, J. E. (1993). *The Rorschach: A comprehensive system: Vol. 1. Basic foundations* (3rd ed.). New York: Wiley.

Exner, J. E., & Weiner, I. B. (1982). *The Rorschach: A comprehensive system: Vol. 3. Assessment of children and adolescents.* New York: Wiley.

Fare v. Michael C., 442 U.S. 707 (1979).

Faust, D., Hart, K., & Guilmette, T. J. (1988). Pediatric malingering: The capacity of children to fake believable deficits on neuropsychological testing. *Journal of Consulting and Clinical Psychology, 56,* 578–582.

Faust, D., Hart, K., Guilmette, T. J., & Arkes, H. R. (1988). Neuropsychologists' capacity to detect adolescent malingerers. *Professional Psychology: Research and Practice, 19,* 508–515.

Federal Bureau of Investigation (1993). *Uniform crime reports: 1993.* Washington, DC: U.S. Department of Justice.

Federal rules of evidence. (1992). Boston: Little, Brown.

Feldman, M. J., & Graley, J. (1954). The effects of an experimental set to simulate abnormality on group Rorschach performance. *Journal of Projective Techniques, 18,* 326–334.

Ferguson, L. R., Partyka, L. B., & Lester, B. M. (1974). Patterns of parent perception differentiating clinic from non-clinic children. *Journal of Abnormal Child Psychology, 2,* 169–181.

Flesch, R. (1948). A new readability yardstick. *Journal of Applied Psychology, 32,* 221–233.

Forsyth, B. W. C. (1991). Munchausen syndrome by proxy. In M. Lewis (Ed.), *Child and adolescent psychiatry: A comprehensive textbook* (pp. 1030–1037). Baltimore: Williams & Wilkins.

Forth, A. E., Hart, S. D., & Hare, R. D. (1990). Assessment of psychopathy in male young offenders. *Psychological Assessment, 2,* 342–344.

Fosberg, I. A. (1938). Rorschach reaction under varied instructions. *Rorschach Research Exchange, 3,* 12–30.

Fosberg, I. A. (1941). An experimental study of the reliability of the Rorschach psychodiagnostic technique. *Rorschach Research Exchange, 5,* 72–84.

Fox, R. E. (1995). The rape of psychotherapy. *Professional Psychology: Research and Practice, 26,* 147–155.

Franzen, M. D., Iverson, G. L., & McCracken, L. M. (1990). The detection of malingering in neuropsychological assessment. *Neuropsychology Review, 1,* 247–279.

Freud, A. (1958). Adolescence. *Psychoanalytic Study of the Child, 13,* 255–278.

Frueh, B. C., & Kinder, B. N. (1994). The susceptibility of the Rorschach inkblot test to malingering of combat-related PTSD. *Journal of Personality Assessment, 62,* 280–298.

Gallegos v. Colorado, 370 U.S. 49 (1962).

Ganellen, R. J., Wasyliw, O. E., Haywood, T. W., & Grossman, L. S. (1996). Can psychosis be malingered on the Rorschach? An empirical study. *Journal of Personality Assessment, 66,* 65–80.

Gardner, R. A. (1992). *True and false allegations of child sex abuse.* Cresskill, NJ: Creative Therapeutics.

Gibertini, M., Brandenburg, N. A., & Retzlaff, P. D. (1986). The operating characteristics of the Millon Clinical Multiaxial Inventory. *Journal of Personality Assessment, 50,* 554–567.

Golden, C. J., Hammeke, T. A., & Purisch, A. D. (1980). *The Luria-Nebraska neuropsychological battery: Manual.* Los Angeles: Western Psychological Services.

Goldstein, J., Freud, A., Solnit, A. J., & Goldstein, S. (1986). *In the best interests of the child.* New York: Free Press.

Goodman, G. S., & Bottoms, B. L. (1993). *Child victims, child witnesses: Understanding and improving testimony.* New York: Guilford Press.

Gough, H. G. (1950). The *F* minus *K* dissimulation index for the MMPI. *Journal of Consulting Psychology, 14,* 408–413.

Graham, J. R. (1987). *The MMPI: A practical guide* (2nd ed.). New York: Oxford University Press.

Graham, J. R. (1990). *MMPI–2: Assessing personality and psychopathology.* New York: Oxford University Press.

Greenberg, S. A., & Shuman, D. W. (1997). Irreconcilable conflict between therapeutic and forensic roles. *Professional Psychology: Research and Practice, 28,* 50–57.

Greene, R. L. (1988). Assessment of malingering and defensiveness by objective personality inventories. In R. Rogers (Ed.), *Clinical assessment of malingering and deception* (pp. 123–158). New York: Guilford Press.

Greene, R. L. (1991). *The MMPI–2/MMPI: An interpretive manual.* Needham Heights, MA: Allyn & Bacon.

Greenfeld, D. (1987). Feigned psychosis in a 14-year-old girl. *Hospital and Community Psychiatry, 38,* 73–75.

Grisso, T. (1980). Juveniles' capacities to waive *Miranda* rights: An empirical analysis. *California Law Review, 68,* 1134–1166.

Grisso, T. (1981). *Juveniles' waiver of rights: Legal and psychological competence*. New York: Plenum.

Grotevant, H. D. (1980). Personality development. In J. F. Adams (Ed.), *Understanding adolescence: Current developments in adolescent psychology* (pp. 110–134). Boston: Allyn & Bacon.

Gudjonsson, G. (1992). *The psychology of interrogations, confessions, and testimony*. West Sussex, England: Wiley.

Gudjonsson, G. H., & Singh, K. K. (1984). Interrogative suggestibility and delinquent boys: An empirical validation study. *Personality and Individual Differences, 5*, 425–430.

Haley v. Ohio, 332 U.S. 596 (1948).

Hammond, W. R., & Yung, B. (1993). Psychology's role in the public health response to assaultive violence among young African-American men. *American Psychologist, 48*, 142–154.

Hare, R. D. (1980). A research scale for the assessment of psychopathy in criminal populations. *Personality and Individual Differences, 1*, 111–117.

Hare, R. D. (1991). *The Hare Psychopathy Checklist–Revised manual*. North Tonawanda, NY: Multi-Health Systems, Inc.

Hare, R. D., Harpur, T. J., Hakstian, A. R., Forth, A. E., Hart, S. D., & Newman, J. P. (1990). The Revised Psychopathy Checklist: Reliability and factor structure. *Psychological Assessment, 2*, 338–341.

Hay, G. G. (1983). Feigned psychosis—A review of the simulation of mental illness. *British Journal of Psychiatry, 143*, 8–10.

Heaton, R. K., Smith, H. H., Lehman, R. A. W., & Vogt, A. T. (1978). Prospects for faking believable deficits on neuropsychological testing. *Journal of Consulting and Clinical Psychology, 46*, 892–900.

Heilbrun, K. (1992). The role of psychological testing in forensic assessment. *Law and Human Behavior, 16*, 257–272.

Herkov, M. J., Archer, R. P., & Gordon, R. A. (1991). MMPI response sets among adolescents: An evaluation of the limitation of the subtle–obvious subscales. *Psychological Assessment, 3*, 424–426.

Hertzig, M. E. (1992). Personality disorders in children and adolescents. In R. Michels (Ed.), *Psychiatry* (Vol. I; pp. 1–11). Philadelphia: Lippincott.

Hess, A. K. (1987). Dimensions of forensic psychology. In I. B. Weiner & A. K. Hess (Eds.), *Handbook of forensic psychology* (pp. 22–49). New York: Wiley.

Hodges, K., McKnew, D., Cytryn, L., Stern, L., & Kline, J. (1982). The child assessment schedule (CAS) diagnostic interview: A report on reliability and validity. *Journal of the American Academy of Child and Adolescent Psychiatry, 21,* 468–473.

Horowitz, S. W. (1991). Empirical support for statement validity assessment. *Behavioral Assessment, 13,* 293–313.

Hutt, M. L. (1985). *The Hutt adaption of the Bender-Gestalt test: Rapid screening and intensive diagnosis* (4th ed.). Orlando, FL: Grune & Stratton.

In re Gault, 387 U.S. 1 (1967).

Johnson, M. K., & Raye, C. L. (1981). Reality monitoring. *Psychological Bulletin, 88,* 67–85.

Kahneman, D., & Tversky, A. (1973). On the psychology of prediction. *Psychological Review, 80,* 237–251.

Kernberg, O. F. (1984). *Severe personality disorders: Psychotherapeutic strategies.* New Haven, CT: Yale University Press.

Kinder, K., Veneziano, C., Fichter, M., & Azuma, H. (1995). A comparison of the dispositions of juvenile offenders certified as adults with juvenile offenders not certified. *Juvenile and Family Court Journal, 46*(3), 37–42.

Krakauer, S. Y., Archer, R. P., & Gordon, R. A. (1993). The development of the items–easy *(Ie)* and items–difficult *(Id)* subscales for the MMPI–A. *Journal of Personality Assessment, 60,* 561–571.

Kraut, R. E., & Price, J. D. (1976). Machiavellianism in parents and their children. *Journal of Personality and Social Psychology, 33,* 782–786.

Kuehnle, K. (1996). *Assessing allegations of child sexual abuse.* Sarasota, FL: Professional Resource Press.

Lamb, D. G., Berry, D. T. R., Wetter, M. W., & Baer, R. A. (1994). Effects of two types of information on malingering of closed head injury on the MMPI–2: An analog investigation. *Psychological Assessment, 6,* 8–13.

Lewis, M. (1993). The development of deception. In M. Lewis & C. Saarni (Eds.), *Lying and deception in everyday life* (pp. 90–105). New York: Guilford Press.

Lewis, M., Stanger, C., & Sullivan, M. (1989). Deception in three-year-olds. *Developmental Psychology, 25,* 439–443.

Lickona, T. (1983). *Raising good children: Helping your child through stages of moral development.* New York: Bantam Books.

Marks, P. A., Seeman, W., & Haller, D. (1974). *The actuarial use of the MMPI with adolescents and adults.* Baltimore: Williams & Wilkins.

Marlowe, D. B. (1995). A hybrid decision framework for evaluating psychometric evidence. *Behavioral Sciences & the Law, 13,* 207–228.

Masterson, J. (1985). *Treatment of the borderline adolescent: A developmental approach.* New York: Brunner/Mazel.

Matarazzo, J. D. (1978). The interview: Its reliability and validity in psychiatric diagnosis. In B. J. Wolman (Ed.), *Clinical diagnosis of mental disorder: A handbook* (pp. 47–96). New York: Plenum.

Matarazzo, J. D. (1990). Psychological assessment versus psychological testing: Validation from Binet to the school, clinic, and courtroom. *American Psychologist, 45,* 999–1017.

Mattanah, J. J. F., Becker, D. F., Levy, K. N., Edell, W. S., & McGlashan, T. H. (1995). Diagnostic stability in adolescents followed up 2 years after hospitalization. *American Journal of Psychiatry, 152,* 889–894.

McCann, J. T. (1997). The MACI: Composition and clinical application. In T. Millon (Ed.), *The Millon inventories: Clinical and personality assessment* (pp. 363–388). New York: Guilford Press.

McCann, J. T., & Dyer, F. J. (1996). *Forensic assessment with the Millon inventories.* New York: Guilford Press.

Meadow, R. (1977). Munchausen Syndrome by Proxy: The hinterland of child abuse. *Lancet, 2,* 343–354.

Meadow, R. (1995). The history of Munchausen Syndrome by Proxy. In A. V. Levin & M. S. Sheridan (Eds.), *Munchausen Syndrome by Proxy: Issues in diagnosis and treatment* (pp. 3–11). Lexington, MA: Lexington Books.

Meehl, P. E., & Rosen, A. (1955). Antecedent probability and the efficiency of psychometric signs, patterns, or cutting scores. *Psychological Bulletin, 52,* 194–216.

Meloy, J. R. (1988). *The psychopathic mind: Origins, dynamics, and treatment.* Northvale, NJ: Jason Aronson.

Melton, G. B., Petrila, J., Poythress, N. G., & Slobogin, C. (1987). *Psychological evaluations for the courts: A handbook for mental health professionals and lawyers.* New York: Guilford Press.

Mendelson, D. (1995). The expert deposes, but the court disposes: The concept of malingering and the function of a medical expert witness in the forensic process. *International Journal of Law and Psychiatry, 18,* 425–436.

Mensch, A. J., & Woods, D. J. (1986). Patterns of feigning brain damage on the LNNB. *International Journal of Clinical Neuropsychology, 8*(2), 59–63.

Mikkelsen, E. J., Gutheil, T. G., & Emens, M. (1992). False allegations by children and adolescents: Contextual factors and clinical subtypes. *American Journal of Psychotherapy, 44,* 556–570.

Millon, T. (1987). *Millon Clinical Multiaxial Inventory–II manual.* Minneapolis, MN: National Computer Systems.

Millon, T. (1993). *The Millon Adolescent Clinical Inventory manual.* Minneapolis, MN: National Computer Systems.

Millon, T., & Davis, R. (1996). *Disorders of personality: DSM–IV and beyond.* New York: Wiley.

Miranda v. Arizona, 384 U.S. 436 (1966).

Mnookin, R. H., & Weisberg, D. K. (1989). *Child, family and state: Problems and materials on children and the law.* Boston: Little, Brown.

Morey, L. C. (1996). *An interpretive guide to the Personality Assessment Inventory (PAI).* Odessa, FL: Psychological Assessment Resources, Inc.

Myers, J. E. B. (1995). New era of skepticism regarding children's credibility. *Psychology, Public Policy, & Law, 1,* 387–398.

National Institute of Mental Health (1991). *NIMH Diagnostic Interview for Children, Version 2.3.* Rockville, MD: Author.

Nemzer, E. D. (1991). Somatoform disorders. In M. Lewis (Ed.), *Child and adolescent psychiatry: A comprehensive textbook* (pp. 697–707). Baltimore: Williams & Wilkins.

Netter, B. E. C., & Viglione, D. J. (1994). An empirical study of malingering schizophrenia on the Rorschach. *Journal of Personality Assessment, 62,* 45–57.

Ney, T. (1995). (Ed.). *True and false allegations of child sexual abuse: Assessment and case management.* New York: Brunner/Mazel.

Nuttall, E. V., & Ivey, A. E. (1986). The diagnostic interview process. In H. M. Knoff (Ed.), *The assessment of child and adolescent personality* (pp. 105–140). New York: Guilford Press.

Ofshe, R., & Watters, E. (1994). *Making monsters: False memories, psychotherapy, and sexual hysteria.* New York: Scribner.

Osgood, D. W., O'Malley, P. M., Bachman, J. G., & Johnston, L. D. (1989). Time trends and age trends in arrests and self-reported illegal behavior. *Criminology, 27,* 389–417.

Pankratz, L. (1988). Malingering on intellectual and neuropsychological measures. In R. Rogers (Ed.), *Clinical assessment of malingering and deception* (pp. 169–192). New York: Guilford Press.

Perry, N. W. (1995). Children's comprehension of truths, lies, and false beliefs. In T. Ney (Ed.), *True and false allegations of child sexual abuse: Assessment and case management* (pp. 73–98). New York: Brunner/Mazel.

Perry, G. G., & Kinder, B. N. (1990). The susceptibility of the Rorschach to malingering: A critical review. *Journal of Personality Assessment, 54,* 47–57.

Petersen, A. C. (1988). Adolescent development. *Annual Review of Psychology, 39,* 583–607.

Pope, H. G., Jonas, J. M., & Jones, B. (1982). Factitious psychosis: Phenomenology, family history, and long-term outcome of nine patients. *American Journal of Psychiatry, 139,* 1480–1483.

Pope, K. S., Butcher, J. N., & Seelen, J. (1993). *The MMPI, MMPI–2, & MMPI–A in court: A practical guide for expert witnesses and attorneys.* Washington, DC: American Psychological Association.

Porter, S., & Yuille, J. C. (1996). The language of deceit: An investigation of the verbal clues to deception in the interrogation context. *Law and Human Behavior, 20,* 443–458.

Raskin, D. C., & Esplin, P. W. (1991). Assessment of children's statements of sexual abuse. In J. Doris (Ed.), *The suggestibility of children's memory* (pp. 153–164). Washington, DC: American Psychological Association.

Raskin, D. C., & Steller, M. (1989). Assessing credibility of allegations of child sexual abuse: Polygraphic examinations and statement analysis. In H. Wegener, F. Losel, & J. Haisch (Eds.), *Criminal behavior and the justice system: Psychological perspectives.* New York: Springer-Verlag.

Rawling, P., & Brooks, N. (1990). Simulation index: A method for detecting factitious errors on the WAIS–R and WMS. *Neuropsychology, 4,* 223–238.

Reich, W., Shayka, J. J., & Taibleson, C. (1991a). *Diagnostic Interview for Children and Adolescents (DICA–R–A): Adolescent version.* St. Louis, MO: Washington University.

Reich, W., Shayka, J. J., & Taibleson, C. (1991b). *Diagnostic Interview for Children and Adolescents (DICA−R−P): Parent version*. St. Louis, MO: Washington University.

Rey, J. M., Morris-Yates, A., Singh, M., Andrews, G., & Stewart, G. W. (1995). Continuities between psychiatric disorders in adolescents and personality disorders in young adults. *Amercian Journal of Psychiatry, 152,* 895−900.

Richardson, G., Gudjonsson, G. H., & Kelly, T. P. (1995). Interrogative suggestibility in an adolescent forensic population. *Journal of Adolescence, 18,* 211−216.

Robins, L. N., Helzer, J. E., Cottler, L. B., & Goldring, E. (1989). *NIMH Diagnostic Interview Schedule, Version III−Revised*. St. Louis, MO: Washington University School of Medicine.

Rogers, R. (1984). Towards an empirical model of malingering and deception. *Behavior Sciences & the Law, 2,* 93−112.

Rogers, R. (Ed.). (1988a). *Clinical assessment of malingering and deception*. New York: Guilford Press.

Rogers, R. (1988b). Current status of clinical methods. In R. Rogers (Ed.), *Clinical assessment of malingering and deception* (pp. 293−308). New York: Guilford Press.

Rogers, R. (1990a). Development of a new classificatory model of malingering. *Bulletin of the American Academy of Psychiatry & Law, 18,* 323−333.

Rogers, R. (1990b). Models of feigned mental illness. *Professional Psychology: Research and Practice, 21,* 182−188.

Rogers, R. (1995). *Diagnostic and structured interviewing: A handbook for psychologists*. Odessa, FL: Psychological Assessment Resources.

Rogers, R. (Ed.). (1997). *Clinical assessment of malingering and deception* (2nd ed.). New York: Guilford Press.

Rogers, R., Bagby, R. M., & Chakraborty, D. (1993). Feigning schizophrenic disorders on the MMPI−2: Detection of coached simulators. *Journal of Personality Assessment, 60,* 215−226.

Rogers, R., Bagby, R. M., & Dickens, S. E. (1992). *Structured Interview of Reported Symptoms: Professional manual*. Odessa, FL: Psychological Assessment Resources.

Rogers, R., Bagby, R. M., & Rector, N. (1989). Diagnostic legitimacy of factitious disorders with psychological symptoms. *American Journal of Psychiatry, 146,* 1312–1314.

Rogers, R., Duncan, J. C., Lynett, E., & Sewell, K. W. (1994). Prototypical analysis of antisocial personality disorder: DSM–IV and beyond. *Law and Human Behavior, 18,* 471–484.

Rogers, R., Gillis, J. R., & Bagby, R. M. (1990). The SIRS as a measure of malingering: A validation study with a correctional sample. *Behavioral Sciences & the Law, 8,* 85–92.

Rogers, R., Gillis, J. R., Bagby, R. M., & Monteiro, E. (1991). Detection of malingering on the Structured Interview of Reported Symptoms (SIRS): A study of coached and uncoached simulators. *Psychological Assessment, 3,* 673–677.

Rogers, R., Gillis, J. R., Dickens, S. E., & Bagby, R. M. (1991). Standardized assessment of malingering: Validation of the Structured Interview of Reported Symptoms. *Psychological Assessment, 3,* 89–96.

Rogers, R., Harrell, E. H., & Liff, C. D. (1993). Feigning neuropsychological impairment: A critical review of methodological and clinical considerations. *Clinical Psychology Review, 13,* 255–274.

Rogers, R., Hinds, J. D., & Sewell, K. W. (1996). Feigning psychopathology among adolescent offenders: Validation of the SIRS, MMPI–A, and SIMS. *Journal of Personality Assessment, 67,* 244–257.

Rogers, R., Kropp, R., & Bagby, R. M. (1993). Faking specific disorders: A study of the structured interview of reported symptoms. *Journal of Clinical Psychology, 48,* 643–647.

Rogers, R., & Resnick, P. J. (1988). *Malingering and deception: The clinical interview: Practitioner's manual.* New York: Guilford Press.

Rogers, R., Sewell, K. W., & Goldstein, A. (1994). Explanatory models of malingering: A prototypical analysis. *Law and Human Behavior, 18,* 543–552.

Rosenberg, D. (1995). From lying to homicide: The spectrum of Munchausen syndrome by proxy. In A. V. Levin & M. S. Sheridan (Eds.), *Munchausen syndrome by proxy: Issues in diagnosis and treatment* (pp. 13–37). Lexington, MA: Lexington Books.

Sanders, M. J. (1995). Symptom coaching: Factitious disorder by proxy with older children. *Clinical Psychology Review, 15,* 423–442.

Schacter, D. L., Kagan, J., & Leichtman, M. D. (1995). True and false memories in children and adults: A cognitive neuroscience perspective. *Psychology, Public Policy, & Law, 1,* 411–428.

Schmidt, J. P. (1989). Why recent researchers have not assessed the capacity of neuropsychologists to detect malingering. *Professional Psychology: Research and Practice, 20,* 140–141.

Schretlen, D. J. (1988). The use of psychological tests to identify malingered symptoms of mental disorders. *Clinical Psychology Review, 8,* 451–476.

Schretlen, D., Wilkins, S. S., Van Gorp, W. G., & Bobholz, J. H. (1992). Cross-validation of a psychological test battery to detect feigned insanity. *Psychological Assessment, 4,* 77–83.

Seamons, D. T., Howell, R. J., Carlisle, A. L., & Roe, A. L. (1981). Rorschach simulation of mental illness and normality. *Journal of Personality Assessment, 45,* 130–135.

Sigmon, S. T., & Snyder, C. R. (1993). Looking at oneself in a rose-colored mirror: The role of excuses in the negotiation of a personal reality. In M. Lewis & C. Saarni (Eds.), *Lying and deception in everyday life* (pp. 148–165). New York: Guilford Press.

Singh, K. K., & Gudjonsson, G. H. (1992). The vulnerability of adolescent boys to interrogative pressure: An experimental study. *American Journal of Forensic Psychiatry, 3,* 167–170.

Spitzer, R. L., & Endicott, J. (1978). *Schedule of Affective Disorders and Schizophrenia.* New York: Biometrics Research.

Spitzer, R. L., Williams, J. B. W., Gibbon, M., & First, M. B. (1990a). *Structured Clinical Interview for DSM–III–R (SCID).* Washington, DC: American Psychiatric Press.

Spitzer, R. L., Williams, J. B. W., Gibbon, M., & First, M. B. (1990b). *Structured Clinical Interview for DSM–III–R Personality Disorders (SCID–II).* Washington, DC: American Psychiatric Press.

Steadman, H. J., McGreevy, M. A., Morrissey, J. P., Callahan, L. A., Robbins, P. C., & Cirincione, C. (1993). *Before and after Hinckley: Evaluating insanity defense reform.* New York: Guilford Press.

Stein, L. A. R., Graham, J. R., & Williams, C. L. (1995). Detecting fake-bad MMPI–A profiles. *Journal of Personality Assessment, 65,* 415–427.

Steller, M., & Boychuck, T. (1992). Children as witnesses in sexual abuse cases:

Investigative interview and assessment techniques. In H. Dent & R. Flin (Eds.), *Children as witnesses* (pp. 47–71). New York: Wiley.

Steller, M., & Koehnken, G. (1989). Criteria-based statement analysis. In D. C. Raskins (Ed.), *Psychological methods in criminal investigation and evidence* (pp. 217–245). New York: Springer-Verlag.

Stermac, L. (1988). Projective testing and dissimulation. In R. Rogers (Ed.). *Clinical Assessment of Malingering and Deception* (pp. 159–168). New York: Guilford Press.

Stouthamer-Loeber, M. (1986). Lying as a problem behavior in children: A review. *Clinical Psychology Review, 6,* 267–289.

Stouthamer-Loeber, M., & Loeber, R. (1986). Boys who lie. *Journal of Abnormal Child Psychology, 14,* 551–564.

Tolan, P. H., Guerra, N. G., & Kendall, P. C. (1995a). A developmental–ecological perspective on antisocial behavior in children and adolescents: Toward a unified risk and intervention framework. *Journal of Consulting and Clinical Psychology, 63,* 579–584.

Tolan, P. H., Guerra, N. G., & Kendall, P. C. (1995b). Introduction to special section: Prediction and prevention of antisocial behavior in children and adolescents. *Journal of Consulting and Clinical Psychology, 63,* 515–517.

Trevethan, S. D., & Walker, L. J. (1989). Hypothetical versus real-life moral reasoning among psychopathic and delinquent youths. *Development and Psychopathology, 1,* 91–103.

Trueblood, W., & Binder, L. M. (1997). Psychologists' accuracy in identifying neuropsychological test protocols of clinical malingerers. *Archives of Clinical Neuropsychology, 12,* 13–27.

Undeutsch, U. (1982). Statement reality analysis. In A. Trankell (Ed.), *Reconstructing the past: The role of psychologists in criminal trials* (pp. 27–56). Kluwer, The Netherlands: Deventer.

Undeutsch, U. (1989). The development of statement reality analysis. In J. C. Yuille (Ed.), *Credibility assessment* (pp. 101–119). Kluwer, The Netherlands: Deventer.

United States v. Dennison, 652 F. Supp. 211 (D.N.M. 1986).

United States v. Frye, 293 F. 1013 (D.C. Cir. 1923).

Walters, G. D. (1988). Assessing dissimulation and denial on the MMPI in a sample of maximum security, male inmates. *Journal of Personality Assessment, 52*, 465–474.

Weiner, I. B. (1994). The Rorschach Inkblot Method (RIM) is not a test: Implications for theory and practice. *Journal of Personality Assessment, 62*, 498–504.

Wechsler, D. (1991). *Wechsler Intelligence Scale for Children–Third Edition: Manual*. San Antonio, TX: The Psychological Corporation.

Weiner, I. B. (1995). Methodological considerations in Rorschach research. *Psychological Assessment, 7*, 330–337.

Wexler, D. B. (1991). *The adolescent self: Strategies for self-management, self-soothing, and self-esteem in adolescents*. New York: Norton.

Widiger, T. A., Mangine, S., Corbitt, E. M., Ellis, C. G., & Thomas, G. V. (1995). *Personality Disorder Interview IV: A semistructured interview for the assessment of personality disorders*. Odessa, FL: Psychological Assessment Resources.

Wiener, D. N. (1948). Subtle and obvious keys for the Minnesota Multiphasic Personality Inventory. *Journal of Consulting Psychology, 12*, 164–170.

Wiggins, J. (1981). Clinical and statistical prediction: Where are we and where do we go from here? *Clinical Psychology Review, 1*, 3–18.

Wilson, J. J., & Howell, J. C. (1994). Serious and violent juvenile crime: A comprehensive strategy. *Juvenile and Family Court Journal, 45*(3), 3–14.

Wrightsman, L. S., & Kassin, S. M. (1993). *Confessions in the courtroom*. Thousand Oaks, CA: Sage.

Yates, B. D., Nordquist, C. R., & Schultz-Ross, R. A. (1996). Feigned psychiatric symptoms in the emergency room. *Psychiatric Services, 47*, 998–1000.

Ziskin, J. (1984). Malingering of psychological disorders. *Behavioral Sciences & the Law, 2*, 39–49.

Ziskin, J., & Faust, D. (1988). *Coping with psychiatric and psychological testimony* (4th ed.). Los Angeles: Law and Psychology Press.

Index

About the Author

Joseph T. McCann, PsyD, JD, is a licensed psychologist and attorney in Binghamton, New York whose clinical and forensic practice encompasses a variety of criminal, civil, juvenile, and family court matters. In addition to being in private practice, Dr. McCann is a staff member of the Children and Youth Mobile Mental Health Team at the Binghamton Psychiatric Center, where he provides consultation and assessment services for children and adolescents placed with various county and state agencies. He has written numerous journal articles and book chapters on psychological assessment, forensic psychology, and personality disorders, and he is coauthor of *Forensic Assessment with the Millon Inventories* (with Frank J. Dyer, 1996). Dr. McCann is also a Fellow of the Society for Personality Assessment. He is on the editorial board of the journal *Behavioral Sciences & the Law* and serves as a consultant to the New York State Office of Professional Discipline and the New York Bar Association's Special Committee on Procedures for Judicial Discipline.